GIRLBOYGIRL

GIRLBOYGIRL
HOW I BECAME JT LEROY

SAVANNAH KNOOP

SEVEN STORIES PRESS
New York • Oakland • London

Seven Stories Press
140 Watts Street
New York, NY 10013
www.sevenstories.com

Library of Congress Cataloging-in-Publication Data

Names: Knoop, Savannah.
Title: Girlboygirl : how I became JT Leroy / Savannah Knoop.
Other titles: Girl boy girl. | Girl boy girl | How I became JT Leroy
Description: 2nd edition. | New York : Seven Stories Press, [2018]
Identifiers: LCCN 2018008349 | ISBN 9781609808419 (pbk.)
Subjects: LCSH: Knoop, Savannah. | LeRoy, J. T., 1980- | Literary forgeries
   and mystifications. | Popular culture--United States.
Classification: LCC PN171.F7 L47 2018 | DDC 813/.6--dc23
LC record available at https://lccn.loc.gov/2018008349

Book design by Jon Gilbert

Printed in the USA.

College professors and high school and middle school teachers may order free examination copies of Seven Stories Press titles. To order, visit www.sevenstories.com/contact or send a fax on school letterhead to (212) 226-1411.

9 8 7 6 5 4 3 2 1

CONTENTS

PREFACE TO THE 2019 EDITION

WE ARE STANDING IN an empty warehouse in Winnipeg, Manitoba, Canada. It is the first day on the set of the movie based on *Girl Boy Girl: How I Became JT LeRoy*. I don't know exactly who is clamoring toward the monitors, I just know that we all are. Later, I will come to realize that many who kneel down toward the light of the screens to take a snapshot with their smartphones are, in form, called Continuity People.

And so am I, I think, obliquely.

A Continuity Person keeps the reality of the artificial world of the film intact, maintains the integrity of the fiction by making sure that glasses don't fill themselves, ashes don't reconstitute themselves into cigarettes, and time works in only one way—forward. In writing this memoir shortly after the experience of embodying JT LeRoy had ended, I had a similar expectation: that the conventions of the form would impose a linear shape to the mass of memory and emotion coalescing and diffusing within me.

I wanted to trace how I had come from point A, agreeing to do a one-time appearance as a fictional alter ego of my brother's partner at the time, writer Laura Albert, to point Q, six years of becoming so deeply entangled with this fictional character and the writer that I could barely think of myself without him or his creator. Writing down the story from memory became a process, not of convincing, thankfully, but of specificity in viewpoint.

This viewpoint is told from the perspective and experience of the object. Yes, I just called myself an object. That's the thing about getting inside of your own meta-world—you become your own disassociated ant moving through space in service to the story, and any detail of your life is always readily available to pluck and plunk into the master script. Sometimes you have to address whether the story is running roughshod over what you want as an actual object in the world. I became used to referring to myself—even existing in—the third-person, which, it turns out, is exactly as liberatory and circumscribed as the first person. I just ran up against parameters in different places.

My story is the story of multiple bodies trying to occupy one body; specifically, Laura and her fictional alter ego JT and me all trying to occupy *my* body. Things get tricky when there is no space. And that is maybe the challenge that kept me coming back for more JT experiences. I wanted to see how much could be housed in this body. At moments, like a chorus, these multiple voices come together to share one consciousness in sync. At other moments, the story holds just one person trying to fit into another's very specific set of terms; another person trying to cram everything they need in the world into another's set of terms. The story, told from memory, ends up being the messiness and complication of two people's intimacy, the constant testing of each other's boundaries. Savannah and Laura's desires fuel the action in the story— why they want what they want, potentially a series of pathologized reasons tethered to the past, becomes irrelevant. It is what they want, in the present and in the future, that keeps them with each other and with JT, and propels them through time. At the moment of the reveal, this tenuous balancing act collapses. When the world crowds in, that is when I discover the limits of what my body can hold.

In writing the screenplay for *Girl Boy Girl*, cowritten with the film's director, Justin Kelly, once again I found myself retelling the story, and felt the changing shape of it under my fingers. Story glitches—an outsized emotion, an unforgettable image, a motivation that once felt so personal and now can barely be remembered—are smoothed and traced over again, transposing memories until the logistics fade and the emotions materialize as one clear trajectory. Stepping away from the cluster at the monitor, I zoom in on the actors' faces on my handheld device—dumbstruck by the familiar yet alien gestures caught on screen, the spazz-out campy stress mouth of Laura's fictional author, JT, the knee bend, the hands up dramatically toward the sky of Laura's fictional best friend/manager of JT, Speedie.

A day and a half before the movie begins shooting, I am driving with my sweetheart, Lee, through the blinding light and low scrub brush of the Badlands when I receive a text from Justin. He wonders if I could make up a few sentences of JT prose for the reading scheduled to shoot the following Monday. As Lee drives, I pull out my old beat-up laptop from the backseat, and stretch my legs up on the dashboard, staring at my socks, feeling absolutely hopeless. A few pithy sentences. That's all. Think about style. Think about . . . emotion. I try to move my mind toward the proposed word puzzle—something that points to the prose, but is not the prose itself. I look out at the side mirror, the plumes of dust rising in the wake of our car. I haven't read the JT books in a while, but they are, to some degree, seared into my brain. There is a part, I mumble, where JT and his mom are on a road trip, and she anoints him as her map reader, and he can't really read the map, but he pretends he can so that he can hold his mother's attention. I look ahead. Fill me up, spirit, fill me with some idea, with *words!* Lee starts to say something about *there is a blade of light, an ashtray flying through the air.* I type rapidly. *And the cigarette butts scattered on the ground,* words dart like small fish from our mouths and we catch them, and transfer them into different vessels, like we are cleaning the water in a fish bowl. The sun has risen to its highest point, and the land shivers around us as if we're surrounded by a lake. *JT, he arranges them . . . in a row . . .* tap tap tap *. . . color-coding them with . . . circles . . . with rings, with lipstick rings . . .* we pour the bright fish back into their bowl. *Each shade a different secret need.* As we hit a main artery road, we speed down the freshly paved highway. Whizzing past the freshly rolled haystacks, we are elated, ready to start another piece of text—Lee blurts out, *My buddy Lucky's got the goods!*

And then abruptly we are pulled over by a cop for speeding. Fuck! The car is a mess, full of crap from both of our lives commuting back and forth between coasts. I look down to notice my seat smeared with chocolate, my feet wading in corn husks (raw corn a favorite of this trip), orange peels, trash, and cracker crumbs. By happenstance we are white, and not by happenstance, the cop lets us move on without too much ado.

That night we get in to Bowbells, North Dakota, and find the number of a woman advertising that she has a few cabins on a lot for rent. There is a constant steady cool wind blowing, like a kiss. In bed with the window open, we hold each other. I lie awake. Now in the night, as the wind floats through the curtains toward our heads, it feels more pressing, insistent, I can feel my anxiety matching it. The winds of memory glitching. Into the future and into the past.

When I wrote the memoir, one of the last things that Laura said to me was, "Just because you played a writer doesn't mean you are one." Looking back on it, I wonder about that. It feels mysterious to me. Writing fiction is a space of possibility for inhabiting different consciousnesses. For impersonation. Is writing only in the saying, or can it also be in the doing, out in the world? Speeding down that highway with Lee, writing under deadline, about to arrive at the movie set, which felt like some approaching mirage, there was something about that moment that felt—not exactly like playing a writer, but like living inside some reality that was not quite my own. Because the proposal of the day had been to write someone else's words, I was free to imagine and to speak with a different voice. I had tapped into the joy of pretending. Joy— which enters suddenly, and then leaves as fast as it came.

Granted, the pact on the "page" between author and reader is quite different from the terms with which individuals out in the world interact. Out in JT land the boundaries are blurry, hard to read, and ever shifting. There might, indeed, be a reason why people don't often "play" with this sort of writing/performance vérité out in the world—and that is that the complete blurring of the lines between fiction and lived experience can fundamentally fuck with you and everyone around you.

There are other versions of the story, from other points of view. I'm *vaguely* certain that art cannot be everything for everyone, and in telling the story as specifically as I can I hope it inspires others toward their own individual perspectives.

Girl Boy Girl is a portrait of a young person's life in which an artist (Laura) upends my core belief system and changes the way I think about the world and the making of art and life forever. My life with Laura, with JT, and many experiences since have shown me that one set of terms does not work for everyone else. Lived experience, felt experience, and imagined experience all combine to construct our idea of reality. The hard drawing of the line between truth and fiction is artificial and will always work to empower some voices and muzzle others, regardless of where the division is made.

I used to feel certain that reality was a complete construction. These days, whether because I have grown older, or because current events in our political climate have gotten so fantastical (with real consequences), I'm not certain. To quote the Savannah character in the movie, "All I'm sure about is that I am not so sure." But every time I revisit this story it reminds me that truth is a constructed reality formed by many sources, that the most pointed moments of reveal are usually a convergence of years of multiple actions, often, a tangle of call and response from multiple parties that rarely fit tidily into a headline or a sound bite.

The following story is told as best as I understood it. Any factual errors are unintentional. When details, names, events, or dates are blurry, I have tried to indicate my sense of confusion. But this is my experience, told to the best of my recollection.

THE RITZ

ASIA ARGENTO AND I were headed for her hotel room at the Ritz-Carlton in San Francisco. As we left Chinatown, I thought about telling the cab driver to switch directions and take us instead to my place down in the flatlands. The taxi accelerated and bit down at each steep crest of hill, the glitter of downtown yawning into the black water of the bay. I doubt she would have approved of my ratty bed, or of my boyfriend, Jonathan, reading a book on the couch.

I'd met Asia in Italy the year before, and since then, I was obsessed. I combed, dressed, and prepared my meals with Asia in a secret chamber of my mind. When I selected music, I wondered whether she would like it. She had a way of snubbing things with such exacting disdain—a flip of her head, a gutteral sound of disgust deep in the throat from the same place that one cries or laughs. I'd abandoned a crocheted wallet and a white leather clutch on the street because once she'd glanced at them with scorn, saying, "You are like an old lady." My face had flushed with embarrassment. But my crocheted wallet and white clutch had suited me, even if they didn't suit her. There was nothing that I enjoyed more than catching sight of an old lady sitting primly on the bus, hands gloved, hat perched, wool suit lint-rolled, on her best foot to the post office or opera. And there were things that Asia wore that didn't appeal to me: lacy, frilly things, not to mention a furry pink bag she always carried with her during those days we spent in Rome. This über-feminine style suited her. She flounced around in stiletto heels and skin-tight jeans scrawled with Bic pen. She could karate kick in those heels. Once I'd seen her hold an ice cream cone in one hand as she thrust her legs in the air, landing evenly back on her glistening crocodile toes. She had just done a voiceover for a schmaltzy action movie with Vin Diesel. After we had gone for a gelato, and I think the excitement of the movie overtook her.

This was the first time Asia and I had seen each other since our time in Rome a year ago, and she would only be in San Francisco until the next morning. I wanted to take her out to eat sushi, show her Dolores Park, and the ruined battlements at the mouth of the bay, with my favorite flight of stairs that fell off into the ocean. My stomach knotted. I hardly knew her, this woman I'd thought about every day for a year.

Without giving a hint of what she was thinking, she glanced at me with heavy eyes then took a drag on her cigarette. Her features seemed to change constantly, looking demure and feminine in one second, edgy and dissolute in the next. The city lights beyond the cab window pulsed against her messy cropped hair. The suspension of the car bounced. I didn't say a word to the driver.

The cab jostled to a stop, and she rummaged in her bag, a Fendi that could have cost as much as my year's rent. It seemed to have replaced her old pink furry thing. Though little known in the US, she was a huge celebrity in Italy. So much so that fashion houses paid her to wear their clothes. She looked at me and said, "JT, you got'ta some change?" Her voice was a growl—much deeper than mine, and I envied its resonance. I combed my pockets. At least I could give her one thing that really belonged to me.

The bellman opened the door. He wore a tailcoat and a turreted hat that made him look like a rook. We traipsed through the lobby. A crystal chandelier drooped from the ceiling, and a red and gold oriental brocade rug hung from the wall. I snatched a green apple from a crystal bowl and caught myself fantasizing about snatching the poor bellman's hat to impress her. Would that impress her? If I were a real boy, I thought, maybe I would do that. But humiliating the doorman was ultimately not a very sexy thing to do. I plopped one, two, three apples into my bag. Not one of the staff even turned a head. My actions became bolder around her, as if I belonged beside her in this world where one never worried about losing socks at the laundromat or tallying the cost of coffee each week. The trick seemed to be to treat one's privilege with indifference.

I was curious to try on the ease that came from money and celebrity, though I didn't think stealing apples from the lobby of a hotel quite qualified. But filching the apples was definitely in JT's character. He was a scavenger, but what was I? Asia bent toward the elevator button console, wrestling her plastic key into the slot. "Got a room on the umpteenth floor," she said playfully.

We shuffled down a long corridor, and I watched her swagger. I was enchanted by her contradictions. She was graceful and almost aristocratic, and yet she could be tough and vulgar. I'd seen her spit on people, throw chairs, and say "Fuck you" with impeccable nonchalance. My attraction to her was a muddle of wanting her and wanting to learn how to be like her. I looked back at the trail of lavender carpet turned against its nap and poked her with a static finger. She tossed me a mischievous grin. I stared at the brass door-knocker, feeling both anticipation and dread. I'd waited for this moment since we'd first met over a year ago—during what was ostensibly my book tour. She'd given me her grandfather's sweater and a vintage Gucci belt. I'd given her a pair of jodphurs, one of my first sewing endeavors. They had brass buttons emblazoned with crowns. And they were too tight in the ankles so they sagged at the butt and constrained that sensitive part behind the thigh. I hoped she would like them, because in truth I had no other gifts to give her. The books were not from me, I hadn't written them. That was what she really wanted: an option for the movie rights to my book, or what she thought was my book, *The Heart is Deceitful Above All Things.*

Too renegade to spend her life kissing the likes of Vin Diesel, she was living up to the legacy of her father, Dario, the renowned Italian horror movie director. She treated me to extravagant feasts—platters of oysters, scallops, and speckled crab claws suspended on islands of kelp. She taught me never to toast without looking company directly in the eye, an ancient Italian tradition meant to detect betrayal. I cringed each time I raised my glass and said, "Salud." She also taught me that when you saw sheep—and we passed a lot of sheep on that trip—you were supposed to flick your finger like there was something sticky on it, to bring money. And when wine spilled you dabbed it behind your ears like perfume. Now, I can't remember why. I had done all of it at her beckoning.

On my last night in Rome, Asia lay down on our rose printed comforter and I began to rub her back, pushing my stubby fingers into her sinewy muscles. I'd inherited my father's hands, short and thick, like an ogre's. Creeper vines on the windows obscured the streetlight from the hotel room, redolent of mildew and frying garlic. The horns and buzz of traffic echoed, making the silence between us more obtuse. She grunted as I pressed into a knot in her muscles.

My sister-in-law, Laura, had been there. She'd watched us sideways as she flung clothes and magazines from one pile to another, preparing to pack. She was the author of JT's books. The process involved re-piling everything while reciting soliloquies. She began packing gifts for her son "Thor," as he was known in JT land. Laura was known as Speedie.

"We got Italian trucks for my little man Thor. My little babyhead. He can make Italian traffic jams. Maybe we can send them tomorrow before we leave. Maybe the concierge can do it. No, I'll probably have to call Simone. Do you have Simone's number, Asia?" Asia groaned.

Although Laura wasn't really talking to us, I was grateful for her ranting. I wasn't quite comfortable with silence. I worried it denoted that Asia and I really had nothing to talk about.

Laura was pale, with knowing eyes, a pointing nose and

chin, and wide curls around her face. As Asia groaned, Laura held onto her stomach through her printed housedress, murmuring, "Oh, you guys are so cute!" Laura had lost a lot of weight since the beginning of our trip, but she was still wearing the same two dresses that I had always seen her in. They hung on her frame loosely like they were someone else's clothes.

I felt Asia's body bristle as Laura said this. As soon as they met, Asia dismissed Laura as the hang-on, the hired help. Every time Laura spoke, Asia had some excluding comment. This time she said, "It's not for your entertainment."

"Are you sure it's not?" Laura said. I felt annoyed, recalling past experiences of friends overshadowing me. Now Laura was acting like she was trying to convince Asia who the real talent around here was. Suddenly I invited Asia to go outside with me.

Laura had insinuated that she wrote JT's books many times. There was even a point in the trip when Laura and I were sure that Asia knew, because after going to Milan together, she offered to put us up in a suite at the "Hotel Laura." In retrospect, it must have been a coincidence.

In efforts to engage Asia, Laura dropped names. In time, she would include Bono, who loved the work. Michael Stipe, who told JT that at a certain point you just had to cut all the fan mail off. Madonna, who spoke with JT over the phone. Shirley Manson, who had written a song for the JT books called "Cherry Lips" and thought that Laura should write her own lyrics for her music instead of JT because it would empower her. The list of JT's admirers was long and impressive. But Asia was not impressed. They were too mainstream for her. While Laura searched for what would grab Asia's attention, Asia would try to pry me from Laura's company. And I would sit in the middle like Switzerland. Back then, I didn't understand Laura; I liked her but I didn't really want to. Obviously I was in collaboration with her so it was better to stay loyal, but I liked the feeling of Asia always beseeching me to come with her alone. Laura didn't drink and couldn't stand the smell of smoke, so Asia would take us to bars. It wasn't hard to convince Laura to go back to the hotel. Laura would take off in a taxi, and Asia and I would hang out and smoke and drink without her.

To a certain degree I could tell that it pleased Laura that Asia and I were courting each other. But there was also a glint in her eye that implied that she hated how I left her out. And it was true. I would remain silently ambivalent when publishers implied that Laura should buy her own ticket to travel with JT. They would put up a slight fuss when we had to stop for her to use the bathroom, or about buying both of us chewing gum. It was easy enough to take their cue and resent her. I was definitely starting to resent that I was pretending to be someone who had nothing to do with me, representing something I hadn't created.

Laura continued with her soliloquy.

"And here is something for Astor. I wish Astor could have come along with us on the trip."

"Yeah," I responded tightly. "That would have been great."

"Astor" was her husband and my brother, Geoff. He made the music for their band. Laura called herself

Speedie, a nickname for her alter ego, Emily Frasier, a Cockney Jew, who had befriended JT on the streets as a teenager and was singing for the band JT had written lyrics for.

Asia's head was down on the bed. I noticed that Laura silently threw an Italian soccer uniform, which Asia had bought for Thor, into the pile to send back home. We had all gone into a soccer shop, and Asia and I had picked out matching maroon and white striped soccer socks. Normally Laura would have thanked her again as she packed up the little uniform. She was always very gracious about receiving gifts. But she didn't say anything.

The familiar impatient feeling of wanting to drop Laura came over me. I felt like Asia and I were always being chaperoned and it embarrassed me. Laura was always censoring my words, vigilantly guarding my true desires and voice.

I told Laura again we were going to go outside.

"You're going to leave me all alone, are you? But don't be gone too long because we still have a shit load of stuff to pack, okay?"

We left the room and had crossed the street into a park with rows of sycamores, pruned so rigorously their branches ended in knuckles.

Once we were alone, I'd wanted to tell Asia that I was not really a transgender ex-prostitute turned writer named JT LeRoy. She must have known. Still, I couldn't sabotage Laura; I held that much allegiance. And there had been something else holding me back, too. I had no idea if Asia was attracted to me—my eyes, the things I said, my preferences and passions—or only to the boy wunderkind I pretended to be.

We ambled slowly through the park. The air was hot and muggy. Asia explained, "You see, these are very old buildings." A few buzzing lamps with gilded poles hedged the cement paths along what looked like a green house, its glass opaque and whitish blue, faintly glowing like larvae. There were bulbs sprouting, what looked dimly like daffodils in flat manicured beds. "And then as you go along the park here there are many ruins. As you pass through you will find hustlers like we saw yesterday." The night before, after dinner, Laura, Asia, and I had driven the long way back to our hotel in her black convertible. As we stopped at the entrance to the park, a few boys and trannys emerged from the dark, some of them leaning on the cobbled stone wall. One of them of fragile build had an earring and razored hair, and a vulnerable way of moving; he was like someone I was supposed to be. I could feel that we all noticed him, though no one said anything about it. He seemed removed from the other boys, as if in pain. Though I would never wish that on anyone, I have to say I felt envious of the way that we all sucked him in. And I thought how strange it can be when you meet some people, you want to devour that person, to consume their story, which seems larger and more profound than your own. At certain points in my life I've wished I were more neurotic, less passive, and emotionally hesitant. I've wished that something extreme had happened to me, which would have made me more extreme. I felt empty and boring. Laura and Asia both had a story.

Long shadows from the trees stretched over the shorn grass. There was an overpowering sweet fragrance in the air. We'd found a marble fountain, and I followed Asia's lead. Sticking my mouth under the lion's head and drinking in the illuminated cold water, I could feel it traveling down my throat. I looked up to the night sky, and counted the few stars muted by the city's lights. And then, as effortlessly as magnetic snaps, we were face to face. Her features blurred as I fluttered my eyes. We kissed. I could hear the fountain's light trickle and an animal moving in the bushes. I felt cold pockets of air above our heads. She had cinnamon gum in her mouth.

Laura came out of her room and called for us, her voice shrill and almost comical: "JT! JT?" We pulled away from each other. I still hadn't packed yet. Asia said in her gravelly voice, "Well, I guess I will see you soon."

I said, "I'll call ya." Thinking in my head, I hope I will call you, but also thinking, someone will call you, and it will probably be Laura.

Asia began to walk away, no maudlin adieus about her.

"Hey, Asia?"

She turned around once more, lightly on her heels.

I continued, "I am really glad I got to meet you."

"Me, too."

Now, a year later, at the Ritz-Carlton, I sat awkwardly on the edge of the bed and yanked at my shoelaces. I kept telling myself that this was my last and best opportunity to tell her about my other life, where I wasn't pretending to be an acclaimed writer. I wanted to tell her, I am Savannah, a twenty-two-year-old community college drop-out. I didn't have any writing to offer her—other than some corny poems. This seemed like the right time. She had her option to JT's novel, *The Heart*. She was going to start writing the script for the movie soon.

I stood up and looked her in the eye. What would she think if I confessed? If she found out how ordinary I was—a girl who cringed at the sound of her own voice, who hated the way she looked—would she still want me?

I loosened my West Virginia accent and said, "Uh . . . I've, uh, been taking hormones for years."

She shrugged and said, "So . . ." Her Italian accent made the word less of a question and more of an opener. I don't think she believed me, but keeping up the lie served our purpose, both hers and mine, and that somehow lessened the absurdity of it all.

"I . . . Uh . . . Well, my sex change is all healed up now . . . It was a . . . a full job."

She gave me a sly smile. I looked down at my feet, my big toe pushing its way out of a hole in my sock.

Then she twisted off her form-fitting shirt and flung it on a chair. She bounced onto the bed and wiggled out of her jeans. She had an abrupt way about her, a very let's-get-to-it attitude. I slowly and self-consciously peeled off my own shirt. I looked down at the ace bandage binding my breasts and suddenly felt very stupid. At least, I thought to myself, I hadn't gotten my period that morning. "See, I got the whole job, but I don't want ever'ee one to know. So I bind 'cause its personal. It's none of anybody's business."

She shrugged again, as if that was fine by her.

I was always amazed at what people would accept from JT—his odd behavior, his passivity, his idiosyncrasies.

Something told me Asia wouldn't have been so generous with Savannah; she hadn't been with Laura.

Asia helped me out of my ace bandage. It didn't feel seductive. I saw JT's onyx reflection in the sliding door of the hotel room, with the bed stand lights shining behind his hunched shoulders.

We both sat on the edge of her bed in our undies: me in my white cotton, she in teasing pale blue lace. A tattoo of an angel spilled across the lower half of her belly, stretching its sepia wings over her hip bones. She patted the cover a little, beckoning me nearer. I looked down at my thighs, which flattened a little as I sat down. They looked huge compared to hers. I brusquely went to the window and swung the curtains shut, catching a last glimpse of us. She was looking at me. She leaned on her palms, one knee bent with her heel digging under her other leg, which hung off the bed. I saw that my pompadour, which I had twisted up so carefully, had collapsed on the short hair around it.

I had been excited the first time I showed her my own hair instead of the blond wig that JT always wore. It was short all around, shorn bangs and a long piece on top, chunks carved out around the ears. It didn't exactly look good; I thought it lengthened the extension to my weak chin, but it was an interesting haircut. That day at Asia's grandparents' house, I beseeched her to trim it, one of my many attempts to be alone with her. Her baby girl, Ana Lou, had also come on the trip. We had spent the afternoon in the sun on top of an arid hill making grass chains. We waited until Ana Lou went to sleep. As she cut my hair I realized it would only take a few minutes. We needed a longer diversion. Just as she finished, Ana Lou woke up. "It's good enough?" she asked, rushing out the door. She was a mother first.

But now, as she clipped her arms under her head and stretched out on the down comforter at the Ritz, there was nothing to stop us. I lay down on the bed beside her, sideways, so close I could feel her heat. She leaned over and grated her teeth against my pale arm, then grabbed my hips and whispered huskily, "I wish I had a dick." I took pause—what exactly did she mean? Was she wishing that she'd had a strap-on? Was it boring to have sex without one? The self-loathing side of my brain told me she just wasn't into girls. In hindsight, I think she was trying to please JT, give him what she thought he wanted. But did she really think I was JT?

At this point the usual roles of who takes the lead and who waits had already been so skewed; things were awkward to start. In many ways I just wanted to get this first time out of the way because I felt so nervous and put on the spot. In the back of my mind I hoped she would invite me to stay with her in LA while she wrote the screenplay for the movie. I saw us having sex on different leather sofas: one cream, one brown, one executive black, disheveled party clothes in piles on the floor, half-full champagne glasses abandoned on the piano. She would dare me into a sexual realm that I couldn't even imagine. I'd had dreams of grappling with her, of kissing and biting her from ear to armpit to toe. I wanted to take her hands—her beautiful hands—and hold them in my mouth slowly like a boa constrictor taking down its food, taking in each crux of that translucent skin between her fingers. I wanted to have sex outside, against walls, on rocks, in parks, in man-made lakes. I'd dreamed of entering her, but it wasn't with a strap-on. In my fantasy, I felt her walls trembling, emanating heat. This abandon would take time for me to work out. I had to let my guard down, and feel comfortable with her.

From my bag, I nonchalantly retrieved a CD, pretending as if I'd just had it with me by chance. Inserting it in the disc player, I said, "You like this?" I couldn't believe that I was living out one of the moments I had practiced so many times in my head.

One of my favorite albums, *Sketches of Spain*, began to play, the austere drum rolls building up into militaristic horns at sunrise. She walked over abruptly to the CD box and shut it off.

"I don't like it."

Embarrassed, I said quickly, "Uh, here, I got'ta another."

The ebbing sitar and harp of Alice Coltrane's *Journey to Satchavanida* recalled rain dripping off the eves, caught in a tropical storm. Did she like this? She nodded. I looked her in the eyes and one last time made a silent pact with myself to tell her the truth, but later. I would tell her the next time we saw each other.

We began kissing slowly. She said, "I'm so shy, JT. I'm not like you think."

I put one hand on the drop of her back between her wings. There she was, just as I had always imagined her. I kissed her clavicle, marveling at the shimmering muscles of her breastplate.

We began slowly to grab, pull, and peel at each other. I slipped my hands around the roping muscles on her back, running my palms down over the dimple of her sacrum and locking my hands together. I wanted to hold onto her for as long as possible. Then she breathed heavily, her thick hair falling in her face. She whispered, "You're beautiful, JT." I shuddered as she said it. There we were, all possibility of disguise or impersonation finally dissolved. In our naked state, I had hoped we would reach a place of honesty and truth. But I felt caught, still wondering whom her words were meant for. I felt JT's passivity—or was it my own?—closing in on me like a velvet curtain, the realization of my fantasies evaporating. There really was no experience—even this most intimate one—that guaranteed authenticity. If Asia knew deep down that there was no JT, she would tire of me quickly and move on to someone who wouldn't be once removed, who wouldn't be fake. If she didn't realize what was going on—if she believed surgery had gotten this good—if she still thought I was a boy who became a girl, still pretending to be a boy—then I wasn't registering at all with her. But that was what I had told her. Either way, I felt trapped.

The following morning, light seeped through cracks in the curtains. In the gloaming, the bed glowed white, shifting like a mirage. The hotel sheets had been tucked so tightly that there were no crooks in which to wrap my feet. Her tousled hair smelled like sweet almond oil, tobacco, and drugstore shampoo. Her face was buried in a pile of pillows and her elbows, tawny and wrinkled like an elephant's skin, torqued out of the covers as if she were poised in a fall. I lifted my hand and pressed it to my mouth, feeling so disoriented that I couldn't perceive the sheets beneath me, just a warm floating feeling.

LAURA

THE FIRST TIME I MET LAURA, I was home on winter break from boarding school. Geoff and she had already been together for a couple of years, but the family didn't get together very often. On this occasion, however, the entire family had gathered for a nonconformist sort of Jewish Christmas dinner at Geoff's mother's house, a modest Victorian perched at the top of Noe Valley in San Francisco, which she and John had purchased in the mid '6os.

A little family history: my father, John, married his high-school sweetheart, Judy, and had three children—Tanya, Michelle, and Geoff. Judy's parents weren't happy about my father being a gentile, so the two of them ran off to Spain. After their funds ran out—his college fund that he had decided to "self-educate" with—my father moved the family back to the States, eventually settling in San Francisco. When Geoff was two, John left Judy for my mother, Sharon, a painting student at the San Francisco Art Institute. Around this time John burned his own writings and began to film things with his sixteen millimeter camera. They went on long trips together to film dunes or hot air balloons. Eventually they moved into a loft south of Market Street. Sharon got pregnant with my sister Hennessey, then me, and John kept working on documentaries. My older sister and I were the children of this volatile union, which was effectively over by the time I was seven.

On the evening I first met Laura, Judy had made an elaborate feast. Not realizing that it was a sit-down affair, our half of the family was extremely late. In addition to her children, their significant others, and our father, Judy had invited Hennessey, her soon-to-be husband Richard, my mother, and me.

Sitting at the lace-clad table, I watched Laura, the latest inductee to our clan. She had a classical look, like a Dutch milkmaid in a Rembrandt painting—with full rosy cheeks accenting her pale skin, thin lips, and cherub's curls peeking out from under her snug brown crocheted hat. She wore a low-cut flower print dress, and her skin was so translucent, I could make out a schema of veins on her chest beneath a row of thin chains.

I noticed that there was a determination in her eating. She shoved food in without seeming to taste it, as if she could have been stabbing her mouth with the fork without feeling it. She wasn't fat, but she wasn't thin, either. At this time, I was charitable in such matters. I had an eating disorder of my own and could recognize kin. I glanced over at Geoff, who sat next to her, munching on a bite of sweet potato. He must have been aware of her compulsions. Later I would see him take care of her, gently telling her she didn't have to eat the whole box of chocolates, it would still be there later.

Geoff was a new-age rock-and-roll health nut, preoccupied with free radicals, exposure to the sun, and airborne germs. (He and Laura shared an obsession about the toxicity of the planet.) Though we hadn't spent much time together as kids, I'd gotten to know him better the previous summer. He'd taken a pizza-delivery gig near my mother's house and would often come by to visit before a shift. He would pick up my guitar and strum away, filling the house with the latest song he'd written. He was passionate about music, and a talented guitar player. He'd wanted to be a musician since he was a child. He'd come of age in the '70s and loved rock and punk, but now he was working on songs with catchy beats and lyrics, trying to write a hit. Geoff seemed filled with the optimism of someone who knows against all odds he is going to make it as an artist.

In those days, he always wore baggy (preferably organic) cotton pants and T-shirts. He spent a great deal of time in his community garden plot growing purple potatoes, fresh basil, and rosemary. In the summers, he picked wild blackberries, which he sold at Rainbow Foods, a co-operative health food store. He also supported his music career by selling Multi-Pure water filters. He generally sold them at swap-meets and by word-of-mouth. With an earnest expression, his eyebrows slightly raised, he would explain how the dense carbon filter on a Multi-Pure removed more lead, more arsenic, and more chlorine than any other filter on the market. He sold one to everybody in our family. One day, so the story went, he got a call from a sultry-voiced woman, who needed her water filter fixed. She'd looked him up in the yellow pages, and now she sat beside him at Judy's table.

Laura told me that she knew Geoff was good-looking from that first phone conversation. He was tall, with wavy dark brown hair and almond-shaped brown eyes framed by a strong brow. His build was naturally muscular and lissome, and he had a loose, buoyant way of moving, as if his joints had coils in them. In the story of their first encounter, Laura confided that in order to keep her block up, she'd told Geoff she was in a relationship with a woman. While Geoff repaired Laura's Multi-Pure—gently screwing back in the filter, checking to see if there was any sediment on the inside of the lid—they connected on the topic of music. They'd both grown up listening to the Dead Kennedys, the Clash, the Sex Pistols, Bad Brains, and the Avengers. Their interests intersected so deeply that he asked her if she wanted to make music with him. In their first session they wrote two songs together.

Knowing Geoff, I can guess how he approached her—being very soft-spoken, he probably kept his head low and didn't look her in the eye. His manner was always sweet and polite. Laura later explained to me, "I mean, I wasn't huge, but Geoff was the type who was coupled up with the pretty girls. I remember that on our first date he put his head on my lap. Even though it was uncomfortable and I was sweating, I refused to move out of that position." At that time Laura was working on her issues, walking her steps of food abstinence.

Judy had disliked Laura instantly. Though I never asked Judy what exactly rubbed her the wrong way, I could guess. Laura clamored for the entire room's attention, whether she was at a meeting or at a dinner party. Part of Laura was always trying to convince everyone around her that she was a force of nature. She was talented, verbose, and smart. She didn't care whom she offended in order to get her point across. She never let anyone ignore her, she wouldn't take no for an answer, and she wouldn't be quiet for the sake of fitting in.

Geoff and Laura had moved in together and started a band called Daddy Don't Go. They supported the music with a phone sex business. Their songs were put on compilations for Internet sex sites, and Laura used her powers of persuasion to get them press in the *Bay Guardian* and other alternative papers. They marketed their music on the street as well. While Geoff waited in the car as the lookout, Laura would plaster freeway underpasses, construction walls, and every pole in sight with their band's posters. Their shows sold out, but they never got signed to a record label. Almost immediately after hooking up with Geoff and starting the band, Laura fell off her abstinence from binging. She hated the pressure of being the lead singer of the band, and had told me once that her eating habits were a pendulum of fasting and binging.

In the candlelight, Laura's fork glinted as she lifted it to her mouth over and over. A row of silver hoops cascaded down her ear. The rest of the clan seemed irritated from having to wait so long for us to show up. Pausing, Laura said to Hennessey, "You know, I just graduated from piercing school."

"Really?" Hennessey seemed relieved to speak about something besides our tardiness.

"I pierced a tongue last week," Laura said excitedly. "There's no other solid muscle you can pierce like that on the rest of the body."

I begged her, "Will you pierce my eyebrows?"

"Savannah!" my mother balked. I'd already pierced my belly button, which made her cry.

Hennessey tried to create a diversion and said, "So, what's going on with the band?"

Geoff said, "Adam, our bass player, had a baby—it's been hard to keep everyone together."

Laura piped in, "But we did this Cyborgasm thing, and that was really cool."

"Cyborgasm? What's that?" Hennessey asked.

"It's this compilation of erotic rock. We only have one song on it," Geoff said quickly, trying not to meet eyes with his mother.

Laura added, "Yeah, it was cool to get a check from Warner Brothers, but they didn't cut us a very good deal. I'm still doing phone sex, you know, for rent."

Judy and Geoff's sisters tensed up. The air was palpably thicker.

Richard, Hennessey's soon-to-be husband, asked, "So tell us, Laura, what's the wackiest caller you've ever had?" Richard was a lawyer and couldn't help but be inquisitive.

Laura giggled a little coquettishly and said, "They're all wacky. Lately, every one of them has been into butt plugs."

"Butt plugs?" Sharon asked, genuinely perplexed. "What's a butt plug?"

Laura said, "You know—it's like a little Christmas tree you put up your butt."

My father, John, leaned back, and rocked slightly on the hind legs of his chair. His cheeks were a little flushed from the wine, and you could tell he found Laura amusing—but he was also sizing her up in his quiet way.

Richard pressed, "There's got to be one caller who stands out, Laura. Come on, tell us about the craziest caller you've ever had."

Laura stopped eating and threw her round eyes up to the ceiling for a second.

Tanya and Michelle, Geoff's older sisters, started to clear plates. Geoff, meanwhile, bent his head sheepishly and cut the remaining turkey on his plate into very small pieces.

"Well," Laura began, "There's my 10 p.m. He's older and from the South, always wants black girls. His fantasy is to be barbecued alive and eaten by a couple of girls at a church social." She transformed her voice, putting on a high-pitched Southern accent, "Now he's on the spit and we sayin', he's stringy, he needs more barbecue sauce on him." Laura's phone sex name was Letisha. What she left out in deference to Geoff's mother and sisters was that Geoff's name was Kaisha—he played Letisha's sister at the church social barbeque. Nevertheless, Judy stood up and went to tend to something in the kitchen. The rage in the back of her throat gurgled into an indignant snort. There was a part of Laura that enjoyed this. I know I did.

After the band fell apart, Laura started writing more seriously. She drafted a story from the perspective of a young teenage runaway, someone inherently sympathetic because of his age and that he survived—she called him Terminator. He was her alter ego who later became JT. Once Laura told me that when she was young she'd always wished she was a boy—a pretty, chosen boy. It just seemed as if boys slid through life easier. No one ever called her pet names. If they called her anything, they were names, like "Fat Albert" and "Witchy Poo," or they were dirty names that made her want to walk faster. As a teenager she would call up hotlines in different voices, transposing her own stories into those of stray teens, mostly boys. Laura would write these stories on scraps of paper, in the margins of newspapers, or on bits of napkins. JT's pain seemed like a metaphor for her own.

Some time back, Laura found Dr. Terence Owens, a therapist who was head of the children's ward at St. Mary's hospital. From what I gather, he was responsive to JT. She called him every day in JT's voice, describing accounts of JT's life, his experiences of traveling around with his mother and living on the street. Dr. Owens told her she should write these accounts down, and offered JT a venue for his work: he would share JT's writings with his social worker class. Laura was thrilled to finish a story and have an audience to read it to. She began staying up all night working on a single piece until it was done. She would ask Dr. Owens what his class thought of the story—did they like the writing, did they respond to those key moments? He could only give her clinical evaluations. She wanted more feedback. She began to seek out other writers she admired and speak to them over the phone as JT. A neighbor put her in contact with the poet Sharon Olds. When she realized she could contact the people who inspired her, she said that it was like calling up God on the phone. She got in contact with the writer

Dennis Cooper and spoke to him regularly for several years. He gave JT encouragement, and connected him to the writer Bruce Benderson, who in turn helped to get JT published. At one point JT and Dennis mulled over the idea of planting rumors that Dennis had actually written the books because JT didn't feel like he wanted to expose his identity. He wasn't ready to put a face on the content of his books.

In those early days, Laura said that JT, who was HIV positive, had Kaposi's sarcoma, a cancer commonly occurring in AIDS patients, which would have been a natural trajectory for a boy who had been tricking on the street as long as he had. Over the phone she would tell people that JT didn't want to go out because he was ashamed of the lesions on his face and body. At this time, she similarly never left the house. She said in an interview when it was all over, "If they can have sympathy for this boy with sores all over his body, then they can have sympathy for me." While the illness functioned to deter certain gay men from wanting to fuck JT, it didn't deter people from wanting to meet him. Of course, when JT would mumble that he couldn't go out because he was ashamed of his lesions, everyone told him, get out there, don't be afraid, you need to live your life. Some people offered to put makeup on him or to be his bodyguard.

Dennis sent JT a picture of his friend, who had died in the '70s as a boy, to put on the back cover of his first book as an author photo. This boy and I, eerily enough, have similar features: a round face and a ski jump nose.

By the time Laura asked me to play JT, his Kaposi's sarcoma had cleared up. Though JT still stayed in the house most of the time and wore disguises when he went out in public, AIDS was no longer part of his story. Laura had dropped it. The boy would live after all—and no one ever questioned it.

In January of 1997, Laura got pregnant. Geoff was trying to get a new band together. Laura took odd writing jobs here and there, and continued to do phone sex for extra money. Their wedding took place in front of a couple hundred people at the Unitarian Church in Noe Valley, when I was away at boarding school. Under the hupa held by four sisters, Geoff and Laura sang a duet of "Our Love is Here to Stay."

Laura gave birth to a boy. She had gained a lot of weight during the pregnancy, and gained even more while she nursed. It was rumored that she weighed over three hundred pounds. She stopped coming to Judy's gatherings. I remember once when Geoff went to the bathroom, a friend confided to us in a ravaged whisper, "How could Laura do that to Geoff?" Geoff made excuses for her as he bounced Thor on his knee. He took Thor everywhere, even as a baby. Hennessey and I would meet them in front of their house to take walks up the hills or go down to the beach. Laura never came out, but sent her love.

I heard from Geoff that Laura had written and published two books, but didn't quite understand the phenomenon until I read them. I devoured *Sarah* and *The Heart* in a day. The whole premise of writing as someone else seemed mysterious and complicated. I thought the writing was beautiful and true, no matter who had written it. Geoff's mother and sisters wanted Laura to publish the writing under her own name. Laura ignored their worries. She had her reasons.

Every senior at my boarding school planned to go to college. At graduation the administration announced who was going where on a thick cream sheet of embossed paper that they handed out to all of the parents. Because I had gone on an exchange program to Thailand my junior year, I was sliding through with the bare minimum of credits and mediocre grades. I'd planned to go to UC Santa Barbara—it was the only school I had gotten into—so that was what I put on the list. But after graduating from high school, I had second thoughts. I was ambivalent about college and very eager to live alone in the city and stay close to my family. My father had recently been in a very serious bike accident and had broken his neck. With occupational therapy, he managed to regain most of his movement. He walked, dressed himself, and drove, but his impaired motor control was comparable to a toddler's, and it was difficult for him to work. I didn't really know what direction I wanted to take in my studies. During the summer after high school, I took Chinese and guitar lessons at the City College of San Francisco (CCSF) and looked for a job, deciding in my head not to go to college.

A few blocks from my mother's house is Basil, a stylish Thai restaurant. Young Thais with tattoos and piercings, who study architecture or design at the Academy of Art, moved from table to table, wielding trays of curry and somtum. At eighteen, I found them intimidating, but I was convinced that this would be the perfect respite from home and school. I picked out which waiters were good-looking, and hoped that they had taken note of me as well. For three consecutive weeks, I dropped off my resume. The owner, Todd, finally called me in. He hired me as a bus girl Mondays through Fridays for the lunch shifts.

The older Laotian women in the kitchen befriended me first. I had lived in Khon Khaen, in the northeast of Thailand, so I spoke their dialect, and whenever I blundered an order and the waiters berated me, it was the kitchen women who defended me. When the pace lulled, they would tell each other's fortunes with Sanskrit cards, or they would take turns sitting on rice bags and invite me to elbow their shoulders, telling me, "It hits a nerve, a very good nerve." They would make delicacies—grilled duck heads, blood sausage, steamed morning glory stalks, green papaya salad with pickled black crabs, and fermented fish sauce with chilis. Eating in their company at the restaurant provided positive food experiences for me. But still, sometimes I secretly binged, telling myself that food shouldn't be wasted, but knowing deep down that it came from feeling incompetent and alone. After work the staff would all have a drink together and play cards. I would join them, momentarily forgetting that I had no idea what I was going to do with my life.

That summer I met a Japanese boy named Hilo at the cafeteria of CCSF. Everyone thought he was a girl, and to be honest that was what originally attracted me to him. He wore baggy clothes and had spiky cinnamon hair. He had a soft voice and long limbs, and his torso was like putty, as hairless and supple as a twelve-year-old's. He said his hormoncs were off. Every time he went to the men's bathroom a man would proclaim, "This is a man's bathroom." I told him he should embrace his ability to float between the sexes. He said all of his friends thought I was a lesbian.

We lasted only a few months as lovers. Around the end of our relationship he became jealous of my relationship with Geoff, who had begun to entreat me to come over to his house and sing songs together. I was excited to do it, but it took me months to work up the nerve. I started taking voice lessons at City, and tutoring with an opera singer.

The first time I came over to sing was on a weekend; I arrived an hour and a half late. As I rang the doorbell to Geoff and Laura's apartment, Geoff rustled the tie-dyed curtain at the base of the glass front door to check my feet, a habit he'd learned from Laura. I took off my shoes and piled them on the stairwell. There were towers of magazines and books, pallets of new promotional energy drinks and healthful snacks piled all the way up one half of the staircase. Laura called from the TV room/phone sex writing office, "Hi Savanni. I'll be out pretty soon."

"Okay," I boomed in a false baritone down the railroad hallway, where, I would come to know, it was always twilight.

Geoff and I headed into the kitchen, passing Thor's latest finger-painted masterpieces, which had been taped up on the dingy walls. I let my finger trail along the embossed decorative metal, and Geoff warned, "I wouldn't touch that—it's got lead. We tested it."

The kitchen was the only room in this long Victorian house that got any direct sunlight, and I squinted from the glare reflecting off the stainless-steel sink. Ice plants in cut-off milk cartons lined the windowsill. I grabbed a mug from the dish rack and turned on the faucet, flipping the switch for the Multi-Pure.

"You know not to run hot water through the filter, right?" Geoff asked.

"I don't think I was."

"No, that's cool. I was just making sure."

"Where's Trev?" I asked.

"He's got a play date until after dinner. The family takes them to the park. They're French, so he comes back saying, 'We played *le football*. And then we had *croissants*.' It's pretty awesome."

Geoff and I went into his office. They lived in a three-bedroom converted into two offices. He had band posters all over the walls and a few portraits of the band from their Daddy Don't Go days showing their floating heads with clunky phones on their ears, the spiraling cords disappearing into a black background. Laura looked straight into the camera with her knuckles covering the receiver, and Geoff's mouth was open as if in mid-song.

Laura came out of her office and sat on the black leather couch, the only new piece of furniture in that house. They had given me a practice tape, which I played at Sharon's in the living room. Sharon had gotten very excited when I would put it on, reminding me over and over that as a child I had said I wanted to be Madonna. As I tried belting out, "When it rains, Oooo" in front of Laura, she adjusted her little brown crocheted hat, standing up to join in. She was passionate about the music and couldn't hold back. She had a great voice, a voice like water. She could do interpretations and impressions of anyone. She could be Swedish, Japanese, Korean, or from the American deep South. Within seconds, she could do a perfect imitation. Her singing voice was strong with a twinge of an English accent. She coached me on the pronunciation of words and how to deliver a lyric. She was enthusiastic and whooped a lot. As I was learning to sing, I got the feeling she was relieved to have this role filled.

Later, when Geoff went to the bathroom, she told me that at our first family dinner she'd spotted my overdeveloped jaw muscles and guessed my eating habits. I felt the shame well up in my throat. I thought no one knew, except maybe another student hearing me throw up in a bathroom at school. My issues with food came from anger and intolerance with myself, and I had no interest in sharing that with anyone else. I was shocked. I mumbled to her that I didn't know what she was talking about. I had never before spoken to anyone about it. Later this would become an important thread in our friendship. She was the first person who I could speak to about my closet binging, denial, and fasting. Late at night, we would call each other after we'd binged. We would pinpoint what emotion we ate out of. I would swear that I would go to Overeaters Anonymous. It took years to finally drag myself into one of those meetings. When I had to admit to a room of people that I was an overeater, my words turned to sand. It just didn't feel right to speak of it. I guess I wasn't ready. In Narcotics Anonymous and Alcoholics Anonymous at least they could talk about the horror days over coffee, cookies, and cigarettes. At Overeaters Anonymous meetings we could barely have tea. I would think, why couldn't I have a drug problem like the rest of my peers? Then at least I would be skinny.

It had started my freshman year at boarding school. I gained twenty pounds. A lot of the girls did. Overeating was the only encouraged vice. Instead of debaucherous drug and beer parties like we were all aching to have, the administration let us have soda and pizza parties. If a prospective student came to look at the school, they brought out brownies, strawberries, and grapes to make it look as if we were treated well. I can remember visiting and cringing at how pimply and claustrophobic everyone seemed. On the weekends we watched serial television and ate Chinese take-out. There was a poster on my first girlfriend's wall of a Calvin Klein One ad with androgynous youths posed with their shirts knotted up to reveal carved hips. My girlfriend was naturally like a rod herself. I developed these complexes that our relationship was not working out because I didn't look like one of these CK One ads. Her ex-girlfriend had been the blade of our school, a senior who always wore a baseball cap and played lacrosse, and was known for coming on to younger girls in the student body. I was too nice, and I was fat, I thought. She broke up with me shortly after we had gotten together.

When I came home for the first time, my mother was horrified. Though she has always been a forward-thinking person, I can remember upon my return her uttering 1950s-type sentiments like, "a woman's figure is everything." When she said the word "fat" she spit it out with the fervor of a comrade giving a People's Party speech against imperialist dogs. That summer my sister and I jogged together, and I would come home and immediately look in the mirror, hoping that I had magically lost twenty pounds. I can remember the disappointment, followed by the desire to eat pizza. Sharon monitored my regiment. If I put butter on my toast she would say, "I don't know if you need that." Hennessey had come back from boarding school heavier as well, and then lost it upon my mother's nagging. Somehow I couldn't talk to Hennessey about what I was feeling. Instead of changing as a result of the negative attention, I just internalized the feelings.

One sunny morning halfway though the summer, I discovered after eating a sandwich that I could stick my finger down my throat and push the button that I had been searching for. I knew it was not a good habit, and I regarded my newfound tool with caution. I tapered off the amount of food I ate, and began to fast except for coffee. I spent as many nights as possible away from home with girls from junior high so Hennessey and Sharon would not notice that I was not eating. These girls all regarded me as a bit of an embarrassment because I was not going to the public high school, I was fat, and I had "turned" gay. On top of all that, I was completely weird about food.

Around the time I started singing for Thistle, Laura lost a huge amount of weight in a short period of time. Afterwards her skin bowed in folds as if one had laid it over her bones to make a fort. It moved like liquid. She had a trick she showed me once we were closer. After a shower, she would drop her towel. Her skin, having never been exposed to the sun, shone like the waxen moon. She pulled in her slender wings and began to oscillate her hips. The skin made a faint flapping. She then picked up speed, throwing her head back, until it echoed off itself, like the sound of a heron beating the water with its wings before takeoff. A survival call. In time, she would adapt to her new body. She stopped wearing the same rayon-printed house dress and Birkenstocks. She would improve upon her appearance in whatever ways she could. "Witchy poo" and "Fat Albert" were gone forever.

Before we started practicing together as a band, Laura had the PR wheels churning. She had a gift, almost a second sight, for understanding what people wanted to hear in the media world. It seemed to be one of her true callings. She never missed the opportunity of promoting herself and her work. Hearing her pitch a story over the phone was like watching the man at the fair spin blue threads of cotton candy until he'd made a dizzy of fluorescent sugar webs.

In the voice of JT, Laura got me into *Interview* magazine to plug the band. JT was on the list of the year 2000's most-up-and-coming hottest people, and in the magazine JT suggested that I, Savannah, should be included on the list, too, as an up-and-coming fashion designer. This was far fetched. I had made my friends a few duct-tape pieces, and myself a backpack out of a paper bag covered in duct tape. Laura relayed to me what she had told them at *Interview*: I was a duct-tape entrepreneur, and when I went out one night, a mob of Japanese ingenues saw me on the dance floor with my duct-tape bag and danced around me, placing special orders on the spot. My brand had taken off, accelerating into a duct-tape kingdom. I was, according to Laura, like the Louis Vuitton of chrome masking tape. So why hadn't they ever heard of me? "That was something they had to ask themselves," she said, out of breath. This sounded like a crock of shit, and I couldn't believe that any one would take it seriously.

When *Interview* called, I had my answers written out. They asked what my fantasy was, and I dutifully answered, "I make duct-tape bags and wallets, but my fantasy is to spray a can of beer on Hansen with me and my brother's band, Thistle." Granted, it was a roundabout way of promoting the band, but it was effective. I went exactly by Laura's script. When a number of people, including my sister and mother, asked what the hell I'd meant by it, I just shrugged. It was the first of many words Laura would put in my mouth. It would have been exhilarating to see my nineteen-year-old face in a magazine, except that I didn't want to show it to anyone. I was embarrassed by the lies.

Interview required a photo booth series of pictures, which seemed easy enough. However, back in San Francisco, Laura had a couple of problems—JT did not exist, and every photo booth in town seemed to have fallen into disrepair since the advent of Japanese sticker machines. Not easily discouraged, Laura called the photo booth company and found one of San Francisco's last remaining booths at a bar in the Mission. All she needed next was somebody to be JT.

Geoff, Laura, and I drove around the bottom of Polk Street looking for young boys. As Laura rolled down her window and stuck her head out, she told Geoff to slow down. She craned her neck to check out a couple of guys standing in front of a Vietnamese noodle shop.

"Honey, there's a car behind me—I can't just brake."

He kept driving.

She pulled her head back in the car and said, "How can I see anyone if you won't slow down?"

"Honey, please, if you knew how to drive you would understand why I can't."

"Okay, okay, we gotta get these pictures to FedEx by seven, so just keep going toward the Mission."

When we got out of the car on Valencia Street, Laura spied a young lesbian couple walking down the street. One of them was wearing a hooded sweatshirt and looked boyish, with a sandy mop of hair sticking out of her baseball cap.

Laura approached them.

"Hey," she said jovially.

The mop-haired one looked at her suspiciously.

"I really like your face, and I was wondering if you could do us a favor. See, I need a photo strip for this contest, it's an art contest, and I'm really shy, so I can't do it myself. Do you think you could go in there with us and take some pictures?"

"I don't think so," Mop-hair replied, looking at her girlfriend. They started walking faster.

"Wait a minute. Wait—I'll pay you fifty bucks. I don't have much money, but I can give you fifty. Come on. It'll take you five minutes. It's nothin'. Fifty bucks for five minutes—that's like doctor's wages. It would mean so much to me, and it really won't be any trouble. You can even keep your baseball cap on."

They seemed to think that we wanted to kidnap them and turn them into sex slaves. Laura kept talking—she didn't leave them a breath of space to say anything. She reached into her pocket and offered some after-dinner peppermints, a handful of which she'd lifted from a bowl at the last restaurant we'd eaten at. She continued, "You just have to wear glasses—you can keep your hat on—I've got them right here, see?" She fumbled in her bag and pulled out bug-eyed shades.

The couple looked at one another. Mop-hair said, "Let me make sure that I know what you mean: just one photo strip for fifty bucks?"

"Yeah. Right on. Right on. Fifty bucks. It's like you found it on the street. Take your girl out for sushi. Or keep it." Laura said excitedly.

We went from the bright afternoon into the bar. It was like entering the mouth of someone who never had dental care; it reeked of old liquor, olive juice, and vapors of something rotting. The dinosaur photo booth was in the back parlor. "JT" went first. She stayed still through each picture. Laura told her to keep her chin down.

The photos popped out of the little chute. They were blurry with streaks of white through the middle. Laura became irate, and strode over to the bar. Geoff's neck seemed to grow shorter, like a turtle shrinking into its shell.

She yelled at the bartender, "Hey, there's something wrong with that photo booth!"

The bartender looked up from the glasses he was rinsing. "Yeah, I know," he said, "It's low on solution."

Laura fumed, "Well, I want a refund. This is outrageous. These pictures are very important, and this, this machine should be maintained. There's an ordinance about that, you know—having faulty machines in public premises. I need a refund. This is not okay."

The bartender looked at her like she was insane. "Well, I don't give refunds for the photo booth out of my till. You can write a letter to the management if you want."

While Laura's back was turned, Geoff paid Mop-hair fifty bucks. She and her girlfriend took off. Laura was still trying to get her $4.50 back while I posed for my pictures as the singer of the band/duct-tape designer. As I waited for the photo strip to develop, Geoff pulled the velvet drape to the side. The machine boiled and spat out my strip. "How'd yours come out?" he asked. They had the same ghost streak across the front. Finally, Geoff grabbed Laura from behind and escorted her out of the bar. "It's not right," she fumed as we rushed to FedEx, just making our deadline to send the pictures out.

Shortly after, Laura started complaining that I wasn't taking my singing seriously, that she knew I didn't have my heart in the band. She resentfully accused me of running off to do Capoeira, a Brazilian martial art, when I could have been rehearsing.

I couldn't deny what was true. After just one class, watching all of these Amazonian woman doing tricks and take downs, I had fallen in love with Capoeira. I shirked school, making sure that I didn't sign up for night classes, and I rearranged my work schedule. I began to stay away from Laura and Geoff, and refused plans with family and dates with friends to take Capoeira classes. Before I went to school in the morning, I packed my uniform and avidly wrote down the traditional Capoeira songs to memorize on the bus ride. I even did my laundry more often to clean my sweaty whites. My dedication showed me something I hadn't known about myself: I was able to commit wholeheartedly to something I truly wanted to do. I had agreed to be the singer in Geoff and Laura's band because I didn't know what else to do with my time. Once I agreed I'd felt obliged to them, but not enough to give them my full attention. I'd let them down. But Geoff told me in his inimitable, sweet way that it was okay. "It's a tremendous commitment. We're bummed, but don't worry. We understand." I felt relieved. I didn't want to be a singer in a pop band.

A few weeks later, Laura called me up and said, "I need you to do me a favor.""What?" I asked.

"I need you to be *him*."

A part of me had been hoping that it would come to this.

"Who?" I asked innocently.

"JT, just once. Okay?"

CHERRY VANILLA

WE TURNED THE FIRST JT TRICK in the old loft on Natoma Street, one of the South-of-Market alleys named after the city's Gold Rush era whores, or so I'd heard. My parents had rented the second-story since 1968. It had 2,000 square feet of unhampered space, originally used as a record factory. The only private areas were one small front room, which had once been an office, a bathroom, and a darkroom installed by my mother. In the big room, sunlight poured through three adjacent skylights onto the pine floors, which were spotted with vinyl tar. At the front of the space stood a pair of freight doors that opened onto the street. An ancient lift waited solemnly beside them, like an old donkey ready to bear its burden down to the sidewalk one story below. I rarely closed these doors, unless it was raining—the place was so drafty that it hardly made a difference. At the far end of the big room, my parents had installed a kitchen, and for the sake of easy plumbing, a shower, too. My mother had painted it with airplane paint, red on top and blue on the bottom; it looked like a puppet theater.

I took over the loft from my father a few years after his accident. He'd tried to continue his life as he always had, but realized that it would be too hard to stay there. The loft was slowly falling apart, and he could no longer repair it himself. It was difficult to get groceries home, and he felt vulnerable walking home at night. So I moved in and sublet the space to three friends. This was at the height of the dot.com frenzy, and rents in San Francisco had gone sky high; we were all grateful for a place to live.

Natoma was crammed with memories from my parents' lives. In the unfinished redwood rafters, my father had abandoned a kayak, an old scuba tank, and hundreds of round metal canisters of old film reels. The forgotten darkroom had been used for storage for years, and one of my roommates and I cleaned out the dozens of tattered boxes filled with archaic camera equipment and ancient chemicals. I was puzzled when I found a squished toad at the bottom of a stack. It was the size of my foot, and I couldn't imagine that my father had let it live in the darkroom. A little disgusted, I tossed it. When I told my mother about it, she exclaimed, "You threw it away? That was the only Valentine's gift I ever gave to your father. I hung it from thread in a blue frame and called it *Sky Piddling*. Did you find the frame?"

For my first JT appearance I needed a good excuse to get rid of my three roommates for an entire afternoon, so I told them that I had answered a personal ad on the Internet: an old man would pay me to bring him to our loft, blindfold him, and let him clean our house. I'd never done things like this, and I could have just said it was a regular date, but a friend once told me a story like this, and I was amused by the idea of a man wearing black socks with yellow woven tips and sock-gators, panting as he scrubbed my sun-bleached floors. It was typical of me to make things as complicated as possible. This part of the lie meant that I had to quickly wash the floors before Laura and company arrived. They were filthy. A fine black silt sifted down through the rafters as I scrubbed them. When I finished, I hurried to the commode and grabbed a mirror my father had hung there on a nail. It was a little rectangle with a cross on it, used for signaling planes in an emergency. I propped it against the floor. I had bought the thickest Ace bandage I could find. It was self-adhesive, scratchy, and a little mentholated. Squeezing my breasts together, I pulled the elastic taut, slowly and painstakingly like a caterpillar spinning his cocoon. I turned to look at my profile. Only a slight mogul remained, and the right clothes could easily mask it. I looked thinner, except for the folds of skin spilling defiantly on to my back and in my armpits. My chest began to burn, but I ignored it and rushed to get dressed. I felt exhilarated. I had figured out how to have no breasts and how to make myself smaller.

I rummaged through my roommate Chuckie's clothes, throwing his neatly folded garments onto the stubby industrial carpet. I looked in his mirror at my profile covering the bandage with my arm. When I did that I looked similar in size to the figure on the cover of *Sarah*, a picture Gus Van Sant had taken of a boy holding a loose red rose. Minus my backside, I was the size of a skinny boy. The ragpicker in me thought that Chuckie's stuff was a little too slick for JT. What I needed was my moth-eaten reindeer sweater that I'd left on the bus months before. I settled for cargo pants and a black long-sleeved T-shirt. When the buzzer rang, I scrambled for my wig and my raccoon-penis-bone necklace, JT's trademark talisman.

Only Laura and the photographer came over. The interview had already been conducted with Laura over the phone. I don't remember what magazine he worked for. He was stocky, but had a boyish demeanor, with slicked back sandy hair and broad shoulders. On first glance, he was the type of white guy that I always judged harshly, unless he seemed gay. Somehow in my mind that would make him seem all right. Laura wore a dowdy straw sun hat with a fake flower tucked into its velvet ribbon over a red wig. A few days before, Laura had taken me to a wig shop down on 26th and Mission. As we tried on different looks, the owner smoothed his greasy tendrils over his shiny head and glared at us from behind his fake wood desk. I picked out a vulgar-looking blue wig. Laura chose Miss Scarlet for herself. In the same way that Laura loved putting on different voices and speaking as different characters over the phone, she loved wearing wigs. She could pick who she wanted to be at any given moment by switching her hair length, texture, and color, though she always wore the same makeup: powder rouge, rust-colored eye-shadow, and light pink pencil.

I nodded to the two of them from behind my mother's reflector bike goggles and blurted out abruptly, "Hi," trying to imitate the low hesitant boy's voice she'd used with me on the phone.

When I opened the door for Laura and the magazine photographer, Laura glanced at me a little searchingly. She said in a British accent, "JT, this is Chris. So, is this place ready for the photo shoot?"

I nodded shyly, trying to croak out a "Yeah." Turning, I ran up the soiled steps, and they followed slowly.

Laura said, "He gets very nervous. You're lucky he didn't puke on you."

"It's an honor to meet you after all this time, JT," Chris called from behind me.

Laura held him back and said in a confidential tone, "Just to let you know, he doesn't like to be touched."

I led them into the big room. I felt a strange sensation of seeing the place for the first time, as if muttering and moving erratically under a wig had given me a new set of eyes. It dawned on me that the place looked like a ward for sick furniture. My mother had long ago stopped visiting because it distressed her to see the place clogged up with junk. Her reaction probably inspired me to bring more junk into the loft. I cleared my throat, managing to say, "Um."

They both sat down. Chris on the green paisley, overstuffed mumps chair; Laura on a scraped-up corduroy. Laura smiled at me—like she was my mother and I was a shy child who needed prompting. She said, "JT, Chris has brought you something."

My torso prickled from the mentholated bandage. I wondered if he could see my back-meat bunching out of the bind. I was struck by the attention JT commanded, although I hadn't spoken a word to this man. I thought about my own life, how so much of the time I tried to fill the silence with smart comments so that people did not assume I was just "some girl." Or else, totally ignore me.

Chris stood and reached out, "Here, JT, I know you like chocolate."

Laura fenced in her cockney, "Chris, ya' didn' bring none fer me? I'm lettin' ya off easy this time. Stand up."

She stood up beside him. He looked confused. She pulled him in toward her and crudely rubbed genitalia with him. I was fascinated, remembering how she'd played the dominatrix on the Cybergasm track.

"Alright. Yer alright. Thas' my test. I'm JT's 'andler, and if I don't get the right feeling around you then I know he can't work with you. No chocolate fer me? That's alright because I am the Fagan I am. He filches for *me*."

We all giggled a little awkwardly.

"You wanna check the place out? See if you got the right shot?" she continued.

"Sure," he said, looking around, "Funky old place, huh?"

"Yeah, s'my sisters. JT thought it suited."

As soon as he went around the bamboo screen that separated my bedroom from the flow of the main space, she whispered in her Brooklynese, "Talk a little more." She gestured with her spindly, pale fingers to my forehead. "Fix your wig."

I'd unconsciously scratched the bangs up to let my scalp air out. The nail-gloss hair made me feel hemmed in, like I was sleeping between the back of a couch and a wall with my socks on and the heater blasting. I pulled the wig down grudgingly, thinking, this is so stupid.

Chris went to the edge of the room scanning the perimeter with a trained eye. He decided to shoot me next to the freight doors. One of the glass panes was held together with duct tape. Chris set down a skateboard decorated with a raunchy picture of a horned woman. He flicked his hand, indicating that I should hop on. I patted down my wig and stepped gingerly. The irony of me pretending to be a boy pretending to be a girl was rich. The gesture was mine, but exaggerated and prissy. Losing my balance as the board rolled, I said, "I, um, I don't know about this, man."

Chris said, "Oh," and dropped his loaded weapon.

Laura squealed from the sidelines, "The mute speaks."

"Well," Chris continued, "can you stand right next to it? Lean it against you?"

I pulled it out from under me and gave it a try: me and the board, a candid portrait of a gutter snipe. Click, click, click—as his shutter beat out a rhythm, I felt more and more awkward. What was this saying? That JT was a skate-boarder? I interrupted his shooting again, "I'm sorry, man. I don't know what it is. I feel kinda stupid. I'm sorry."

"Okay. I'll take the board out, and we'll do it like that. I thought it would be a good prop, but that's okay. Alright. Get loose," he said, dropping it behind him. It landed on its side, and the top wheels spun loudly as if they had gravel in their axles.

Laura stood in back of him, indicating with her own chin that she wanted me to lower mine. She considered it my most recognizable feature. Lower the chin. Lower, the, chin. Lower.

"Get loose!" Chris repeated, clicking away. I stared down at my sneakers.

"You got small feet, JT."

Did boys ever have feet this small? And where was my Adam's apple? I wondered why I was worrying. Laura was only paying me what I would have made in one shift at the Thai restaurant. Plus, she'd offered to get me a bikini and chin and upper lip wax. It was quintessential Laura to hone in on one's soft spots. The truth was I did want that wax. Once when I was twelve, I'd enticed a popular blond boy over to my house with my mother's Camel unfiltered cigarettes. We languidly lay in my bed together, enjoying the summer heat and trying to blow smoke rings. He was curious about my bra straps. Our date was going well. And then all of the sudden, he sneered, "You're the bearded lady. You've got a chin like a lumberjack!" I had vaguely noticed a few hairs sprouting from my chin but not until he said this did it go on my fast-growing list of things I needed to change about myself. I kicked him out of my bed and vowed to get some tweezers and never to speak to him again. Only recently have I decided that I like the hair on my body.

I reminded myself that I wasn't just doing this for the wax; I was doing this because Laura and Geoff had asked me to help them. And when had I ever had the opportunity to do anything like this? It wasn't that big of a favor, dressing up as a boy—I dressed like a boy all the time. Though it seemingly had no bearing on my life one way or the other, I suddenly felt compelled to try to impersonate JT's character as accurately as possible.

I said, "Uh. I was stunted."

Laura added, "He's actually part dwarf."

Chris laughed, taking a few more pictures without putting his eyes to the viewfinder.

"I'm like a big monster compared to you," he leered. (Laura often intimated that JT had given head to reporters because he couldn't distinguish between the attention for his writing and the more familiar sexual attention he used to get from tricking.)

Chris snapped a few more pictures and said, "Alright. I have another idea, and tell me what you think. I brought . . ." He stopped clicking and changed his film adeptly with one hand, the camera propped on his knee. "I brought some lipstick. I was thinking maybe you could put it on while I shoot you."

Laura whooped, "That's hot. That'll be great. Fucking great."

Chris asked, "Is that alright?"

I took my hands out of my pockets. I knew what he wanted: a flippant, gay boy bending erotically towards the mirror. In my real life, I applied drugstore lipstick with my pointer finger. I said, hesitantly, "Okay, I can do that, I guess."

"Yeah? So let's go in front of the mirror."

We filed through the labyrinth of blinds and sheets back to the main space. Passing my room, Laura said off-handedly, "My sister's room. She's in London right now."

I touched my throat as if to quiet the smooth part where a bump should have been. Why did she say that? She was pulling me out of JT.

Chris asked, "Where do you live, JT?"

I thought, he's checking up on our facts. He doesn't believe us.

Laura answered for me, "We live in the Mission."

I frowned at her. Why hadn't she better prepared me? Wasn't it obvious when she answered for me?

"Hey," Chris said suddenly, "Can we shoot it in your bathroom?"

I cringed.

"Oh uh, hold on," I said, thinking, make voice lower. I bolted ahead of them and picked up the mirror I'd been using earlier to adjust my bandage and returned it to its nail hook. No evidence. Then I surreptitiously snapped my bandage, the motion similar to pulling out a wedgie. My breasts were numb.

Behind me, Laura said, "He barely ever goes out. He's like a zombie. Just stays in the family room writing. Gets chocolate stains all over 'is keyboard. You know, he stays in the same pajamas for weeks at a time. We finally said 'Listen, bloke, you can't be smellin' that way 'round our child.'"

They looked at me.

I said, "Who you talking 'bout?"

He handed me the lipstick. I flipped it over. The label read, "Vixen." I leaned in and fumbled with it.

He said, "Alright, cherry, vanilla, and go!"

I felt as if my body was caving into itself.

"And beautiful, very sexy," he said excitedly.

My reflection looked awkward, my nose too bulbous and my cheeks too fat.

He said, encouragingly, "Stunning!"

I heard Laura ask in back of him, "Can he keep that lipstick?"

The stick, rolled all the way up, crumbled off its hilt

and plopped down onto my sneaker. Laura laughed; Chris snapped away.

"We done?" I asked trying to drawl a little. I felt exasperated that she was just standing there laughing. Did I look as stupid as I felt? I felt like I had failed at being a graceful fairy.

"Ah, I think we got that shot."

Returning to the big room, Laura said to Chris, "You know, you really should bring me chocolate next time. I won't forget." She fixed her hands on her hips. Chris distractedly jogged through his Polaroids.

"Can I have one of those?" She asked, her voice raising its pitch like an auctioneer's.

"Yeah. Here, take this one."

"That one? And this one?" She insisted, teetering back and forth a little.

"No, I can't give you that one. It's my marker."

"Well how 'bout I trade you this one and that for that?"

"Here, I'll give you these two."

"But you'll be sending us the pictures too, right?" she asked with urgency.

"Yes."

"Right on. At ease," she said. He winked collecting all of his gun-black gadgetry into its rightful pockets. "JT, adieu." He went to hug me, but I winced. "That's right. I understand. Real honor to spend time with you, man." He turned. "Speedie, also an honor. I'll remember your chocolate in the future."

"You better or else the Gods will whip you in your sleep every night 'til you do."

"Bye," I whispered.

From the landing, we watched him tromp down the long steep stairs, his equipment banging at his sides. He waved once more and shut the door behind himself.

Laura waited a moment as if she was counting his paces and said, "Fucking great. Just fuckin' great."

I said, still trying to practice my drawl, "I can't do that accent. I think he knew."

"No he didn't. It was fuckin' perfect."

"You should have given me more details. It looks obvious when he asks me where I live and I can't give a straight answer." I cast the blue rat's nest off my head and started to scratch violently. "I need to get this thing off my chest. I think they're going to shrivel up and die."

"Here, I'll help. Let me see the chocolate . . ." As she examined the label, she said, "They don't care. Those details don't matter. People believe what they want to. I've noticed all these years, if I'm speaking with someone and I established myself as someone else, I can drop my accent completely after a while and nobody ever notices because who they think I am is already ingrained in their conscience. People rarely question what you tell them. Why should they? I rarely do. So those details, unless it's a very blatant fuck-up, don't matter. And even then I'll be beside you. You did great."

"I know they don't matter because this is a one-time thing," I snorted, peeling my shirt off, unhooking the butterfly clips on the ace. The bandage stayed intact and stiff as wet pants put out to dry in a snow storm. I flung it near her lap. She helped me in the back, clutching the chocolate bar.

She read the percentage of cacao and muttered, "Dressed up Hershey's. They all think JT is a pansy." Once the bind was shed, I lumped it on the sofa. The thing reminded me of skin grafts and pickled body parts in jars. My tits felt like bruised, imprinted lumps, and I quickly pulled my T-shirt over them.

She asked, "Can I look in your kitchen?"

I nodded yes. This would become a ritual for us whenever we entered someone's home.

I walked with her, rubbing my chest for circulation. Neighbors' conversations floated up through our safety-glass windows. One naked light bulb reflected off of the Formica counters, which I'd scrubbed a few hours earlier. This was a welcome relief from the usual trail of crumbs, coffee stains, cigarette butts, and pats of butter that my household left around as a collective sacrifice.

She opened our dank fridge, and I felt her disappointment. Naomi only ate vegetables, fish, and rice. I insisted on buying Swiss chard that I never cooked. The boys had nothing but greasy jarred condiments and a box of Jiffy cornbread mix. I fished an orange from the back shelf and handed it to her. We leaned on the counter and looked out into the dark open space. The sheets, which partitioned my roommates' personal spaces, undulated in the breeze from the open freight door. I watched as she peeled the orange. Her overextended left thumb bulged on one side. As I learned later, every night before she went to bed, she popped it in her mouth, hooking her pointer finger over her nose, often proclaiming, "Time for a cigarette."

She said, "You know, I think you just needed to get warmed up."

I replied, "I'm not cut out for this."

"You did fuckin' perfect."

I fell silent.

We scissored the orange pulp, chewing on the rinds, while waiting for her cab.

Twenty minutes after she'd left, my phone rang. As was her habit, she began by asking, "Are you on a landline?"

"You know I only have one phone and it's cordless."

"You need to get a land line."

"I don't think you have to worry," I said irascibly. "I am perfectly happy without one."

"So listen," she cleared her throat. "I've got another meeting. In two weeks." She described the impending meeting with Gus Van Sant.

"Will you dye your eyebrows blond? I'll make you an appointment and you can get another wax on the side. One of those Brazilian thirty-five dollar jobs."

"Why do I need to dye them?"

"It's a good disguise."

This made no sense. Certainly, I would be more noticeable walking around with peroxided eyebrows. I repeated, "This was a one-time thing . . ."

I could have quit. There was a part of me that wanted to, but I was also intrigued. Pretending to be JT was like starting a love affair. I felt energized even during the most mundane parts of my day.

The next day, setting up for the lunch rush at Basil, I allotted lemon rinds to rows of perspiring ice waters and replayed the best moments of the photo shoot in my mind.

I ended up dying my eyebrows blond, and my hair, too.

HAUTE CUISINE

EVEN THOUGH I WAS ALREADY LATE, I decided to get a cup of acrid coffee from the Mr. Pickles deli. Ignoring the endless ringing of my cell phone, I popped my bike's front tire up on the curve and stopped before a plywood plaque of Mr. Pickles himself. He was painted the same lewd green on both sides, and wore a sombrero and a gun-belt loaded with "MUSTA," the R and D having long ago worn off. My phone rang again, and I glanced at the pad. It was Laura calling, again. I had already spoken to her about fifteen minutes before. She was nervous because Gus Van Sant, the director, was coming out to talk about optioning JT's novel *Sarah*. He was bringing Mike Pitt, an actor who had been discovered on the street and had recently become a teen icon after his stint on *Dawson's Creek*. I was nervous, too. I slammed the coffee, surrendering to my slight hysteria. I flattened the paper cup, threw it in a waste bin, and jumped on my bike.

I rang the doorbell to Geoff and Laura's apartment. Swinging open the door, he said sweetly, "Hey, you're here."

He had on black jeans and a paisley shirt, which he'd unbuttoned to reveal his smooth mid-chest. This was a lot flashier than his usual corduroys and sweatshirt uniform.

"You look so handsome," I said.

"Yeah?" he said, "I was worried about my hair."

"No, no. You look good." I said, walking up the stairs. "I'm sorry that I'm late." Late and apologizing after the fact, as usual.

"That's alright. We're not ready anyway. You want something to eat or anything? Laura's still getting dressed."

"I'll take a glass of water."

Laura called out in a small voice, "Savanni, can you come here for a minute?"

Moored in the middle of the bedroom was a king-sized mattress, heaped with snarls of covers, clothes, and laundry. One side of the room was lined with built-in drawers and cupboards. Fruit-patterned curtains obscured the only window on the far wall, lending the room a greenish tint. Laura, dressed in her customary shapeless flower print, was leaning into the closet, tossing chunky sandals in various hues onto the narrow strip of floor between her and the bed. One could almost measure the importance of the impending meeting by the height of the pile. If *Sarah* got made into a movie it might mean no more dim, crappy apartment, no more day-to-day money worries, a few of Geoff's songs on the soundtrack, and maybe even a record deal. The unfathomable potential made me want to dive into the porto-closet alongside Laura and start chucking shoes in the air with her. I waited for my marching orders—what she and Gus had discussed regarding the option, details of their friendship, what she'd said to Mike Pitt to convince him to come out along with Gus. I confess that my apprehension was also fueled by the fact that I was a huge fan of Gus's since I'd first seen *Drugstore Cowboy* at the age of thirteen. I'd watched it over and over, memorizing lines. While Laura disappeared into the rickety closet, I scanned the bed for a hat, the hex of hexes.

"What do you think? These?" she muttered, holding up a pair of the same sandals in black.

I said, "Sure."

She then walked out into the hallway and placed them at the top of the stairs. I waited in the doorway of the bedroom.

"Geoff," she said a little more shrilly than before, but still gently, "Did you take out the car seat yet? We've really got to get out of here." She looked at me a little desperately and said, "Here, can you help me?"

I obediently followed her back into the kitchen. From behind a sarong curtain that hung before the pantry, she retrieved two Neiman Marcus shopping bags. She said proudly, "I found these in my neighbor's recycling bin." She began packing them with bottles of olive oil, fancy chocolates, chili jam, gummy-candy hamburgers, fortune-telling fish, and two bona fide Cheat River mugs, just like in the novel *Sarah*.

"Wow, the Cheat River."

"Yeah, I got them just in time."

"So, what did you want to tell me about Gus?" I asked carefully.

"Gus, right. God, I am sorry I am so scattered. Ah."

"It could be any little detail. I just don't want to go in cold."

"We talked about, um, the option, but I said I wasn't sure, so just say that. You can leave it open. And I talked to Mike briefly over the phone, and he sounds, real, sort of, displaced. He wasn't sure what coast we were on. But there's a sweetness to him."

I frowned and said, "Something else?"

She said, biting the edge of her thumb, "Let's see, I'll think of more."

She led me to the top of the stairs, pulled on her shoes, then handed me the wigs. I placed the red one on her head, adjusting it so that it was straight. She looked so fragile and pale with all that scarlet nylon hair framing her face. She'd lost a lot of weight in the past couple weeks since we'd done the Cherry Vanilla shoot. She donned a straw hat with a little white flower in the band. I carelessly yanked at my blue wig and slid on my glasses. Geoff plunked the car seat behind the front door. He leaned against the banister, rocking his thumb and pinky back and forth like an incessant drum roll, and asked, "You guys ready?"

Geoff hovered in the white zone in front of the hotel. Glancing in the rearview mirror, he pulled at his bangs, trying to conceal his receding hairline. Our father had been officially bald by the time he was twenty-nine, so considering that, Geoff wasn't doing too badly. He was only thirty-three, but he knew that if he was going to make it as a musician it had to be soon—nobody was giving any breaks to balding rockers. Meanwhile, Laura dialed Gus's room number on her cell phone and told him in JT's southern drawl, "Hey y'all, we're down heere waitin'."

In the backseat, I repeated under my breath, "Down here waitin'. Heere waitin'."

Mike and Gus crashed into the backseat like a wave. Mike squished in the middle, and Gus leaned over Mike to shake my hand. I bowed my head, extending my right hand limply, growling almost inaudibly, "Hi, hi." I was certain that my voice would give me away. I imagined Gus saying to himself, "This doesn't sound like the same person I spoke with a moment ago on the phone." After a few seconds of awkward silence, Mike grabbed my shoulders and said coaxingly, "You don't have to be shy with us. Here, I brought 'choo something." His cheeks were flushed, and his lips bright fuchsia as if someone had painted them. Frank and Chuckie, my roommates, would have swooned over his sulky boyishness. His features were delicate like a doll's. His malapert hair hung over his misty blue-green eyes. I felt jealous that he was the authentic reformed urchin—Mr. Real-life Oliver Twist. At the same time, I couldn't help but be charmed by his good looks.

Out of his knapsack, with a magician's flourish, he pulled a white mesh thong with lace trim the color of Spanish moss, cut for packing, and a matching cupped bra, cut for stuffing. I felt the heat of my blush burn my cheeks.

Laura, turning around in the passenger seat, whooped, "That's hot, fucking hot." Then she retrieved the Neiman Marcus bags and pushed them into the backseat, saying in her cockney accent, "Look, JT brought you presents too!"

Geoff pulled out into traffic as Gus and Mike took inventory. Gus held up the pepper jam and nodded at me approvingly while Mike pulled out the gummy burger packages and, tearing them open, whispered to me, "You white-trash bitch!" Laura kept herself wound-up in her seat and said, "So, Gus, Mike, I'm Speedie," then pointing to Geoff, continued, "And this is Astor, my partner."

"Yes, JT has told me about both of you—it's a pleasure to finally meet." Gus said.

"Been talkin' about us JT, have you? Hope he didn't say anythin' embarrassin' about Astor here!" And she nudged Astor's arm with her elbow, implying all sorts of sordid connections that I didn't want to even begin to consider about my blood.

"JT told me many wonderful things about you both," Gus reassured.

Geoff cleared his throat awkwardly, nodded in the rearview, and asked, "So this your guys' first time in San Francisco?"

In a reserved voice, Gus replied that he'd visited before. He propped up his head with his hand, leaning his elbow against the closed window. He wore a plain postal-blue crewneck sweater and a pale-beige collared shirt. He had a tiny frame and a big head with sandy overgrown brown hair. His eyes were deep amber like tree sap. As he explained that he had been living in Portland for a long time, he didn't look at Laura or Geoff directly, but watched the scenery outside the window. I thought of one of my favorite scenes in *Drugstore Cowboy*, when the Matt Dillon character is high and has fantasies of escape—rabbits, spoons, and keys blowing past the white light of the backseat window. I wanted to ask Gus if he'd compiled the soundtrack for the movie himself, but I figured that JT wouldn't ask such a toady question. Meanwhile, Laura and he talked about the astronomical prices of Victorian homes in Noe Valley. I marveled at how she kept the conversation constantly flowing.

We drove up to Twin Peaks. The sky was a naked blue. We looped down the other side of the hill and headed to the Presidio while Laura kept talking, pointing out her favorite houses. I kept quiet, sighing occasionally, my head drooping like a dehydrated flower, my hands folded in my lap. I felt Mike staring at me. I stole a few glances myself, feeling as if I was in junior high, making gooey eyes with one of the popular boys. His leg pressed against mine with gentle pressure imposed by the backseat. Finally he said, "You don't have to be shy with me, JT. Will you let me see your eyes?"

I opened my mouth a few times like a guppy.

Laura pounced.

"Go 'head, JT, show 'im your eyes. Go on. You 'eard 'im. Don't be shy."

I whispered dumbly, "I uh, I don't uh—" I knew I sounded like a girl.

Gus watched me curiously. Mike, his mouth opened slightly, scratched his ankles with his long fingernails (alarmingly long, I thought) and pressed, "Come on, JT."

I shook my head back and forth, feeling the wig wag. With the intonation of Eeyore, I said, "Alright." Here I hadn't even said a word, and I didn't feel like they were doubting my intelligence. My silence was endearing. I pulled my bike glasses off hesitantly and dramatically, blinking like a daunted baby rodent. Here they are, I thought, the windows to my perfidious soul.

Laura gushed, "Aren't they beautiful? Isn't 'e angelic?

You could see why 'e needed protection on the street. 'E's just so delicate. Can you imagine the throngs of men around 'im?"

Geoff laughed at her exuberance.

Mike said, "Yeah. You have pretty eyes, JT. Why're you keeping those hidden?"

Because it's a disguise, I thought to myself.

I couldn't tell what Gus was thinking. He was very contained. I could feel him taking it all in, enjoying the bizarre silence that followed. I cracked my window. Geoff speeded us through the Cyprus-lined byways of the Presidio, the same route I took on my daily bike ride. The grass and miner's lettuce along the road were still lush from a month's rain. We passed the boarded-up insane asylum. I thought to mention something about it, but laughed a little to myself instead.

Heading out to Sea Cliff, Geoff drove by a beige stucco mansion. Laura shouted excitedly, "There's Robin Williams's house!" She twittered about how he had read the books and sent JT a really sincere message about them.

We parked by a steep cement stairwell leading down to a small beach that looked like a murder scene in a Hitchcock movie. Gus said in a pleased tone, "Here. This is the place. Let's do some pictures here."

I wrapped my neck and chin in a grey knit scarf. The five of us gathered along the metal railing and leaned over. The waves below sucked up the black-pebbled beach. The Pacific Ocean stretched beyond. Tufts of foam drifted up through the air like dandelion fluff. They clung to the steps and coyote bush.

"I've got to get a picture of all of you," Laura said, leaning her hip out to fish through her dirty black bag. She pulled out her disposable camera and made us block together. "Alright, *Mozoltov!*"

Mike put his arms around Geoff and me. Gus kept his arms folded and stood aside.

She looked at him and asked, "Am I stealing your shot?"

"No, I don't mind waiting a bit," he replied.

"Right then, get in," she said, ushering him along with a flick of her hand. She hopped a little in her place, and I could tell her feet were cold in her diaphanous stockings and stout sandals.

Gus sidled hesitantly up to Geoff and stood with his arms still folded. Laura pulled her chin down and gave me a meaningful look, then she snapped three consecutive shots.

Mike shivered and said, "Let's go. I'm freezing my balls off up here."

"Yeah, me too," Geoff agreed.

Following them down the steep, pock-marked cement stairs, I catalogued this balls expression for future use.

The black pebbles of the beach crunched like new snow underfoot. Doomed baby jellyfish reflected the cold winter sun. Gus directed me to stand in a ravine of driftwood. Blue Styrofoam, bleached plastic bottles, an ancient clock, and a blender adorned the smooth, twisted branches. I lifted my hand against my cheek to hide my "Marilyn" piercing above my lip: a beauty queen in a state of false surprise. Geoff and Mike watched, bracing themselves against the wind, their heads tucked into their necks like a couple of roosting birds. I stood frozen with hunched shoulders, what was fast becoming my signature pose.

After shooting about twenty pictures of this same pose, Gus said, "I can tell this makes you uncomfortable, JT."

I nodded. Gus fussed for a moment with the F-stop on his camera.

Laura walked up to me and whispered, "Ask him if you can raid his minibar later, okay?"

I shooed her away.

Trying to project my voice over the wind, I turned to Gus and said, "My balls are real cold." Had he heard me? It didn't seem like it. I tried again, "My cold balls are about to freeze up."

Without acknowledging my comment, Gus said, "I'll take some pictures while you go up the stairs."

Mike caught up to me and we scaled the steps in time with one other.

"How long?" I said, my breath growing uneven from the ascent, "How long were you on the street?"

"A few years . . . And you?"

I had no idea how long I'd been on the street. I thought he might swap stories with Gus later and it wouldn't add up. I said, "She saved me. And Terry, my therapist. I don't know where I would be without them."

"Yeah," he said, giving Laura a glance.

I kept my hands behind my back, one hand wrapped around my other wrist. This was the way I had often seen my mother walk up the stairs. Hearing the clicking of Gus's camera, I quickly slid them into my pockets.

"Hold it right there, JT," Gus instructed. He took a few more pictures of me looking down at my sneakers.

I trembled and chewed on my lips, hamming up my discomfort.

Mike laughed, "You really are a spaz, JT."

I smiled a little demurely at him. Swiveling toward Gus, I said, "Are we done yet?"

"Let's go eat!" Laura said.

Gus looked at his watch and said, "Well, our reservation isn't for another hour, but I guess it doesn't matter."

Rubbing his hands together obsequiously, the maître d of Charles Nob Hill greeted us, "Monsieur Van Sant, we are so pleased to have you this evening." He assessed the rest of us with a little dismay and said, "Please, follow me. I have your table ready for you."

The maître d led us from the waiting room into an elegant dining room with a barrel-vaulted ceiling. Its walls were lined with sumptuous leather banquettes. The kitchen was enclosed, and two doors swung back and forth on their squeaky hinges as tuxedoed servers hurried to take care of the three other parties ensconced at opposing points of the room. The maître d swept his arms graciously to a round table in the middle of the room. We passed a middle-aged couple. She had shoulder-length dyed-blond hair and wore a knitted Chanel suit. He had the ruddy complexion of someone who enjoyed his cocktails and wore a pink oxford, a blue blazer with gold buttons, and a Rolex. They reminded me of some parents of the girls I'd gone to boarding school with. They glanced over their menus and took stock as we passed by.

I started to sit. The maître d pulled out a throne-like chair and waited for me to take my place. I sat down quickly and then stood up like there was a pin in the cushion. I grabbed Laura's hand and whispered low, "I gotta' go take a leak." I was rather pleased with my improvisation and headed for the door with a gold silhouette of a portly gentleman.

The maître d eyed me and said, "No, Madame, this is for monsieurs." I tightened up my neck up and blustered, "I *am* a boy!" hoping that my table had heard me, and remembering how Hilo, my ex, used to look when people mistook him for a girl. I glared at the maître d and pushed the door open forcefully to punctuate my feigned offence; I would have to thank Hilo, if I ever saw him again.

The bathroom smelled of talcum powder and cologne. The French wallpaper depicted repeating gold scenes of sheep and oak trees, little boys, shepherds, and women with bustles. I sat down on the pot sighing as I did my business. Even after I'd finished, I sat there for a while, wondering what it would be like to pee standing up. I washed my hands in the gold basin and dried them with one of those thick paper towels that are somewhere between paper and fabric and always feel like a waste to throw away. I pulled off my glasses and cleaned them with my damp towel, just to get a little more use out of it. A red indentation severed the bridge of my nose. I flipped over the empty gilt trash-can and stood on top of it. My butt looked big in powder blue corduroys with rubbed out knees and frayed hems. But the shirt was good, a '50s plaid pajama shirt with heart-shaped buttons. I'd tried to pick clothes that emulated the look of the boy in the author photo on the back of *Sarah*.

It felt strange, trying to look like a ghost. I ripped the wig off, closing my eyes for a second. I began to vigorously scratch my scalp, telling myself again that this evening of excess could be fun, couldn't it? I'd gone to boarding school and I was aware of upper-middle-class rules—you don't talk about money or ask personal questions or beg to raid minibars. I knew what fork to use for my salad and what spoon to use for my soup. Without the wig, Savannah could have sat down with that conservative couple and probably charmed the pants off of them. No. I yanked my blue wig back on. It was much more interesting to join forces with Laura and Geoff and forget all the conventions, proprieties, and inhibitions that could truss me up in a modern corset of mediocrity.

Returning to the table, Laura asked, "JT, do you want fish? I'm having the whole chicken. I'm pregnant, you know." She directed this last bit to Mike.

I laughed without meaning to. I'd never used the "I'm pregnant" excuse; I usually used "I haven't eaten a thing all day."

Mike giggled, "Wow, I didn't know." He'd taken off his sweatshirt and was wearing a striped T-shirt worn down to a gossamer. I could see the blond woman and her husband at the next table sucking him in, repulsed yet fascinated, as if they were watching porn or a car accident.

I said, "I think I might want the pork chops."

Geoff cringed, "Ugh, pork."

Laura scolded, "You don't eat pork, JT! Astor," she said to Geoff, "You're going to get the fish, and, JT, you'll have the quail, and I'll have the chicken. That settles it. Oh my, look at Gus reading the wine list just like it's the holy scripture!"

He held his wire-rimmed glasses like a monocle over one eye.

"Mmm," he hummed. "They have a lot of really good wine."

A stocky busboy with slick hair and a priest's collared shirt arrived bearing a basket. He kept his tongs poised, a starched white napkin draped across his arm. He visited each of us, leaning ceremonially to reveal the contents of the basket. The bread was arranged from white to dark. "Fig, sour, levain, and black olive," he repeated softly, as though he were reciting a liturgy. Then he took his tongs and gracefully set the bread on our plates. When finished, he back-stepped, bowed his head, and somberly reassembled the remaining slices into a continuous arrangement.

Gus said to Laura, "What do you think, Speedie? Chateau Lafite? A Pommard? A nice Burgundy, perhaps?"

She flashed him a charming grin, "Is that the pink bubbly? Do you think I know the first cluck about wine? JT is the one with the refined palette. 'E's the one who put me up on the *bonne* chocolate. Though I can remember a time when he was eating Snickers bars. Now look, 'e's all uppity from his talent!"

"And I'm draggin' you along with me, Speedie," I said. Fun, this was fun.

Gus grinned indulgently while Geoff leaned into me and said with knit eyebrows, "You aren't going to have those porkchops, are you? You shouldn't eat that stuff. I mean, this is a real high-end restaurant, but I don't see any awareness on the menu about their meat being free range. Those chops could very well be from Porkshwitz. I'm going to check to see if that fish is wild, otherwise I might have to say I'm a vegetarian."

Suddenly, the head waiter appeared and announced, "Oysters Rockefeller. *Bon appetit.*" A cohort of five servers delivered each of our party a heavy porcelain soup spoon with a dollop of something green and slimy topped with a sprig of parsley.

Without further formality, Mike slammed the whole thing like a shot of tequila, clanking the spoon on his teeth.

"Yeow," he bellowed. He sanded his tongue with his napkin. "That tastes like snot! I think I cracked a tooth."

The voyeurs at the next table shook their heads disapprovingly.

Gus looked at Mike affectionately and lamented, "*Pauvre.*"

Mike swallowed a big gulp of wine and insisted, "You can't tell me it didn't."

Laura agreed, "It did."

Geoff said, "Shellfish and everything like that makes me queasy. I like California rolls. The avocado and rice kind of back it up—but this stuff. Just looking at it makes me queasy. In fact, I can't eat mine. Do you want it, Mike?"

"No, dude, you eat it. That's not fair. That shit is gross. You haven't been tortured like the rest of us. The chef made it special for you, too. Astor, eat it."

Geoff laughed, "No, I can't."

The bread priest returned to the table.

Laura said, "Don't eat too much bread, you guys. Don't want to fill up on carbs."

Mike said snidely, "Okay, Atkins-South-Beach Speedie."

Laura giggled, "Right on," and grabbed five pieces of bread, tying them up in her napkin. She batted her lashes coyly and said, "May I have another napkin when you get a chance?"

As the bread priest retreated, Mike reached back and grabbed a few slices from the basket. The affronted bread priest stuttered then abruptly stalked off.

Laura screamed, "Now you have ruined my chance of getting another napkin from that man, Mike!"

"I'm sorry, what did I do?" he asked, brandishing the bread between his teeth like a wild dog.

The head waiter cleared his throat. Laura initiated, "I'll be havin' the chicken and my little friend 'ere will be 'avin the quail and 'e'll start with a smoked salmon. Astor, love, you gonna 'ave the fish. Let's see, and I'll start with a salad. I think we should order a few things for the table too—one of those artichoke souffles and maybe one of those scallops au Corsica? Astor, love, what'll you be startin' with?"

I took a deep breath and bit my tongue as I stared down at the menu. At the bottom it said: Three course *prix fixe* $189. Laura reached out and touched my arm in a motherly way. She whispered, "I'll share my chicken with you."

Mike yelled across the table, "JT, you're so shy. Why don't you let go a little?"

I shrugged, realizing that he was staring at me seductively with those soft blue-green eyes of his. I felt baffled and glanced at Gus, who was laughing a little under his breath. Mike leaned further over the edge of the table, nearly knocking over his wine glass, and said, "I want 'choo to hear my music, JT. You'll like it."

I said, "Um, I would like that."

"JT, I feel like we came from the same place."

Laura said, "I feel like you two did, too."

Mike strained a little further across the table. "Do you want to go sneak a cigarette with me?"

"Fucking great," Laura said, throwing up her hands. "JT shouldn't be smoking, 'cept between meals! You all go on, then." She patted my shoulder encouragingly.

I cringed—what would I do on my own? What would I possibly say to him? I looked from Mike to Gus to Mike again and muttered, "Okay, let's go have a cigarette."

Sheltered by a hunter green awning, we tumbled down the steps, smudging up the brass banister with our buttery fingers. Dense hedges framed the tall '30s high rise. I could hear the far-off hum of cable cars. Mike tucked a Camel between his pouty lips, then expertly flicked his pack so as to offer me one. He cupped his hands and lit it, then took a long drag, gazing at me all the while. He passed me the lighter, and I fumbled with it, wondering what I was going to say to him. His eyes were on me all the while, and I could taste his exhaled smoke on the back of my tongue. I felt that intense insecurity that always ensues right before a kiss. I swallowed uncomfortably just as the heavy door swung open at the top of the landing. Suddenly, Laura burst out, clutching her disposable camera. I couldn't believe how relieved I was to see her, to hear the bubbling of her phony cockney.

She pointed accusingly, "Aha! I've caught you: smoking cigarettes and getting dirty fingernails! You look disreputable! You should be ashamed of yourself, you there with your dirty wig!"

I raised my stubby hands and displayed my chewed-up fingernails. She continued, now pointing at Mike, "And, you, you with your lipstick!"

Mike exclaimed, "I don't wear lipstick, Speedie! My lips are just like this!"

Laura said, "A likely story! JT did a photo shoot last week for the first time and he put on lipstick. It was fucking brilliant! And you didn't fuck the photographer. I was so proud of you, JT." Then she said in a conspiratorial tone as if I weren't there, "He used to have sex with anything that paid him a compliment."

"Really, JT?" Mike said, "I can't imagine you being, like, that forward."

"It was more like resignation. Like a dog rolling over." Then, holding up her camera, she said, "Can I take a picture of you two together smoking?"

Mike asked, "Why're you always taking pictures?"

"Because JT's my family. And you guys look very sweet together."

Mike put his arm around me and leaned his head into my neck.

Laura said, "That's beautiful!"

I held my cigarette flamboyantly, blowing the smoke out with a push of breath, the way Chuckie and Frankie did when they brought a date back to the loft. I affected arabesques, lifting the cigarette up and down and up again to my lips.

Laura said, "Why don't you guys kiss each other?"

Mike and I smelled each other's cheeks, then pecked on the lips like children. Laura clicked her shutter. The flash sounded like a doppler, rising in pitch.

Mike said nervously, "But you've got to be careful because I don't want this to get back to my agent."

Laura winked and giggled dangerously, "I can see the headlines now: Teen heartthrob hot for JT LeRoy!"

Mike gave Laura a that's-not-funny look.

Laura said, "Don't worry, we wouldn't actually do that."

"But you were in *Hedwig and the Angry Inch*?" I countered.

"My agent definitely didn't like that." Mike turned to me, "But I loved your books, JT. So they can fuck off."

Laura and I smiled at one another, and she said, "Let's get back to dinner!"

As soon as we sat down, with the assistance of the maître d, who insisted on pulling out my chair for me, the waiters presented our appetizers. They had to rearrange a few bread plates to make room for the extra souffle and scallops. I gobbled up my salmon in a few bites, ravenous from the afternoon spent in the cold air.

Geoff smiled at me and said, "I wish Hennessy were here. She would really enjoy this."

Alarm bells trilled in my head: how could he mention our sister's name so nonchalantly?

Laura licked her spoon and groaned, "Delicious." She winked at Geoff and blew him a kiss. He laughed easily and grabbed at the air for it.

Next, the cohort of waiters proffered a lobster custard with caviar, which was received much more graciously than the chef's previous snot appetizer. I felt my cheeks grow rosy from the wine. When the entrees arrived, we dug in with gusto, though after a few bites I felt my little-boy underwear begin to pinch at the waistline. I continued eating anyway. Laura passed vegetables to Geoff.

Gus turned to me, "Are you happy with the restaurant choice, JT?"

"Gus," Laura said, "It's a pleasure he has waited for all of his life. Here, JT, try Astor's fish." She quickly switched our plates.

I glanced down at the fish, white with tiny grey veins running through its flesh. Then I looked up, "Thank you, Gus. It's all real beautiful."

Laura leaned over to me and said in a loud whisper, "Ask him if you can raid his minibar."

I clenched my teeth and hissed, "Not right now."

"Of course, you can raid my minibar, JT. After dinner," Gus said.

I said with embarrassment, "Did you hear that?"

Pointing her long finger, glistening with chicken juice, Laura said, "You're very indulgent, Uncle Gus."

"That is one of my strengths," he said in an assured tone.

The servers swept up our plates and deftly scratched all the crumbs from our white tablecloth. The head waiter, meanwhile, recited a long list of desserts. As I listened I felt as if a dam were bursting inside me. "The Grand Marnier souffle sounds yummy," said Geoff. "I want the warm chocolate thing," said Mike. "The pomegranate grapefruit sorbet," said Gus. Suddenly Laura exclaimed, pointing to me, "It's this young man's birthday. Will you bring us a special taster of everything on the menu?"

"Madame?" inquired the head waiter.

"A taster," Laura repeated, "Of everythin' you got."

"One moment, Madame, and allow me to consult with the pastry chef."

"Oh," she said, "And can I have a double mochachino?"

"Madame?"

"Or no, make it a 'ot chocolate and a pot of green tea with soy milk on the side."

"We have no soya, Madame."

"God damn, old-world milk then. Does the cocoa come with whipped cream?"

"Yes, madame."

"Right on!" she exclaimed.

Gus ordered a grappa.

I was still a little tipsy from the wine, but I boldly announced, "I'll have one, too."

Gus smiled encouragingly.

It came in a tiny silver glass and smelled of rubbing alcohol, searing my throat as it went down, warming my stomach when I swallowed.

Then from behind I heard the rattle of a cart, and as I turned, Laura lost her cockney and moaned, "Hell yeah!"

Geoff and I laughed.

The waiters brought silver bowls with scoops of ginger, chocolate, and pear ice cream; slices of tart, brownies, chocolate cake, caramelized sugar spun into fans, souffles, and a three-tiered tower of petit fours with glazed kiwis and orange rinds. Each time they presented a dish, Laura yelped, "Hell yeah, this is the life, JT. You keep writin' books."

I snorted without meaning to.

Gus, his fingers loosely curled around the stem of his grappa glass, watched us descend on the desserts with our silver spoons.

I thought to myself as I scraped away at a piece of brandied chocolate cake that I would like a memento of this dinner, a spoon perhaps, something small. I stared across the table and Mike caught my eye. As if reading my mind, he shaved a little ice cream onto to his spoon with one hand, saying, "This is yummy." With the other he snatched a silver pinecone decoration into the shadows of his lap. He winked at me.

The table was a battlefield, with the desserts decimated, the only survivors being a few petit fours. Everyone leaned back in their chairs, trying to breathe a little room into their waistlines. Gus requested the bill, and a distended silence fell over the table. I fixed my gaze on the mosaic mirrors decorating the candle-holder, wondering if I should offer to pony up for the tip—though even that would have been way out of my league.

From her old black bag, Laura retrieved a purple leather glove, which she stretched languidly over her long fingers. She opened and closed them a few times, grasping the air. The gesture seemed symbolic of so much in her—her desire, her strength, her struggle to be the person she knew was inside her that no one else would see. She raised her hand like a conductor and announced, "Let's guess the amount of the bill."

Gus was sitting a few feet back from the table. I wondered if he would be offended by this, but he didn't seem to be. He crossed his legs and stacked his hands on his lap. I knew she wasn't trying to offend him—she just couldn't help herself. He tilted his head a little, and an inchoate grin crept into the corner of his lips. He said, "Go ahead."

She squinted and said, "We 'ad the wine. See my problem is I don't know anythin' about wine."

He said, "Those were two nice bottles of wine."

Mike said, "Nice. We know what that translates to."

Laura said, "Nothin' but the best for you, JT."

Mike shouted, "Six hundred and fifty-two dollars and some odd cents."

Laura countered, "I think that's too low."

Geoff said, "Eight hundred and thirty-three dollars."

Gus said quietly, "I won't give you any more hints. I am going to let you guess until you're satisfied. Then we will look. This is without the tip, mind you."

Laura and I glanced at each other.

I said in a timorous voice, "Sixteen hundred and nineteen dollars."

She mimicked me perfectly, "Sixteen hundred and nineteen. See, JT knows the price o' things. I say, sixteen hundred and fifty."

I could hear everyone in the dining room listening to us. The doors to the kitchen ceased their squeaky swinging.

Gus said, "I guess seventeen hundred."

"You could buy a real fancy cardboard box for that," I murmured.

Gus slid the black leather check folder toward the center of the table, then lifted its top slightly as if demons might fly out of it. He squinted dramatically and announced, "Sixteen hundred and—it's a toss up. Should I say who was closest? Sixteen hundred and forty. I believe you are the winner, Speedie."

She puffed up with pride and said, "Mum would be proud. Yeah!"

Gus tucked a golden credit card into the folder, and the head waiter swooped down on it, saying, "Thank you, Monsieur Van Sant."

We all chimed in, "Thank you, Gus."

He beamed back at me, "I'm glad I paid you a visit."

COPACABANA

AFTER A SPRING SEASON OF JT EVENTS, I felt like it
was consuming my life. I had skipped out of so many of
my own commitments that I had run out of excuses. There
were book signings, interviews, and two important photo
shoots, one with Mary Ellen Mark for *Vanity Fair*, and the
other with Steven Klein for the Icon issue of *Pop Magazine*.
Wanting to experience something on my own, I decided to
go to Rio de Janeiro, to participate in the Abada Capoeira
International Games and workshops. The thought crossed
my mind that if I liked Brazil I would never return home;
Laura would have to figure out how to make JT work all by
herself. And I would have my life back.

About halfway over the Caribbean, I realized that I had
forgotten my address book, in which I'd written all my
Capoeira contacts. With my Portuguese consisting of little
more than "hello" and "where's the beach?" it would be
difficult to find Marcia, my teacher, in a city of millions.
I suddenly despaired. What was wrong with me? A cre-
scendo of voices echoed in my head, of people in my life
that I had disappointed. I began to make a list of things that
I would change about myself: I would stop eating, I would
meditate, I would be in control. I would get my fucking life
together. I would be good at something, and it would have
nothing to do with JT LeRoy.

All of these thoughts, however, didn't change the fact that I would soon be landing in a foreign city with no place to go. As we began our descent I scanned through my guidebook and picked out the cheapest hotel in Copacabana. I practiced saying to the taxi driver, "*Copacabana Fazendina, por favor.*" Suddenly a burst of bossa nova riffs and girls in '60s bathing suits and high heels on the beach danced in my head.

I checked into the hotel and slept for a day and a half. When I awoke, I felt an overwhelming sense of loneliness. I threw off the polyester pink-and-blue coverlet and walked over to the window. Outside stood a mountainous heap of rubble, a construction project appearing as if it had no completion date. Was this a sign about my own life? What would I do with myself if I couldn't find my Capoeira group? Why did I always plan so badly?

I hadn't eaten for almost two days, but I didn't like to eat in restaurants alone. I decided to fill my time by going to the beach. When I went down to the lobby, the woman working at the front desk informed me that the hotel offered a complimentary continental breakfast. In the center of the dining room stood a banquet table arranged with plastic trays of cold cuts and slices of white cheese rolled tightly with toothpicks, glistening sesame buns and mini croissants, slices of papayas, oranges, pineapples, and bunches of tiny purple grapes. I drank three cups of black coffee and rolled a cigarette. I enjoyed it with the zeal of one who is never allowed to smoke indoors. I thought, if Laura had been here I wouldn't have been able to smoke. We would have eaten and eaten, and then been too torpid to go to the beach.

Feeling adequately caffeinated, I stepped out onto the street. The air felt warm and slightly humid. I gazed down the long avenue between the high rises and could see the blue horizon of the Atlantic. If I was going to the beach, I needed to get a Brazilian wax. I had heard about how the Brazilians scoffed at spidery gringos. Strolling down the street lined with knotty balboas, I thought about how Laura would have hated it here. It was too hot. She always wore a wig and a hat, tights and long shirts that covered her arms. She lived in fear of contracting skin cancer, smearing her nose and cheeks with thick grainy sun-block. Buses caterwauled through the lanes, and thick brown smoke chugged from their exhaust pipes. As I walked by a man popping corn at his painted stall, my stomach groaned violently from the smell of caramelized sugar and margarine. People walked quickly past me. The women, regardless of their age, wore their hair long and dressed in tight clothes. They wore bold colors: fire-engine red and lime green. I had once dressed more like this. My teenage years had been spent trying to make myself fit conventional expectations of how a woman should look. I'd had a bottle-blond bob. I'd worn high-heeled platform shoes, wraparound dresses, and tight jeans. But I had never really felt comfortable. The few boys I dated made me feel socially inept. And the experience of losing my virginity with a Thai man named Beer still makes me cringe. During my senior year of high school, my best friend cut my hair short, and I vowed never to have long hair again. It put me out of a certain kind of circulation, and that was fine by me.

As I strolled, I realized that I hadn't seen a woman with

short hair yet. I wondered what the Brazilians thought of me. Back home, I got the sense that some people (especially older ones) dismissed me as peculiar. A few weeks before my trip, I had been waiting for an elevator and an elderly man, also waiting, turned to me and asked, "Do you use the little girl's room or the little boy's?" "The little girl's," I replied as the elevator doors swung open. I stepped in. He stood staring at me, and I reached to hold the door for him. "That's alright," he said, "I'll take the next one."

Not everyone was confused by my gender. And not everyone was fooled by JT. When I met Mary Ellen Mark, she knew right away that I was a girl. And the interesting thing was that I had taken great pains to cover up my gender with her. For every outfit on that photo shoot, Laura and I had stuffed my tights with a sock. In his billowing full-length tutu, JT was not only girly, he was very well-endowed.

When we had our final meal together, Laura, Mary Ellen, and I had all sat close, sharing entrees and drinking wine. Mary Ellen squinted and flipped a braid over her back saying to us, "You know, I have hung out with many transgendered people over the years. But you don't *feel* like a boy to me. And you don't seem to me like you've come from the street."

Laura rushed in with a response. "I know! I know! I agree. That's the amazing thing about JT. He really is unusual in that way. His spirit is not like a boy. He is a different kind of being." I watched Laura play with the stem of her wine glass.

Mary Ellen gave her a knowing look.

"But I don't feel even the residue of a boy. JT, you just don't *feel* like a boy to me."

What should I say to this? It seemed pointless to lie. "I am, and I am not." I said hesitantly.

Laura roared, "Soon he's going to get his holy fucking period!"

I walked up to a salon that was packed with honey-skinned women laughing and gesticulating to one another, and decided that it was as good a place as any for my purpose. As I opened the door, bells rang.

"*De sculpe. Voce tem* . . . ?" I said, making the gesture of ripping cheesecloth mid-air.

The woman at the desk stared at me as if I were an idiot and bellowed, "Mariela!"

Mariela came out, her candy-floss heels with rhinestones lightly tapping across the granite tiles. Again, I went through the motions to explain myself. She was very tan with sprinklings of freckles on her face and shoulders.

At first she stared quizzically, then exclaimed, "*Ah, depilação, minha filha.*"

She ushered me into a little room with fake wooden panels and fluorescent lighting. I had a sour stomach from the coffee. There was a piece of waxy paper laid out on a recliner. I kept my eyes on the ceiling, which looked as if it had been sprayed with cottage cheese, and we struggled through some small talk—where I was from, my name, how long I would be in Brazil. I felt awkward as I tried to communicate, laughing a little too loudly. She coyly clucked at my baggy panties. I shucked them with a kind of resignation. Maybe, after my wax, I'd get myself a thong. All the Capoeiristas wore them to practice. And

I could see the lines of Mariela's beneath the nylon fabric of her pants.

Under the fluorescent lights, my skin appeared sallow and white. On my forearm, black hair sprouted out of a mole and a pinkish purple scar. Mariela gummed a glob of wax out of a small silver pot with a flat stick. She hummed under her breath. Then she smoothed the sterile pale violet goop over my upper thigh as if she were icing a cake. Unlike the aestheticians in San Francisco, Mariela used no cheesecloth. My stomach growled.

One of the hardest things about being JT was that I had to relinquish control over how I represented myself and allow Laura to create me. My bleached eyebrows had finally grown in brown. Frosty highlights remained on some of them. No one ever even saw JT's peroxided eyebrows because I always wore long bangs and dark sunglasses that swallowed up my face.

I had recently done a big photoshoot with Steven Klein, who had asked, "And the sunglasses? Do you think they could come off?"

"Absolutely not," Laura said.

I shook my head rapidly from side to side.

"Before we left, JT said, 'Speedie, remember something for me. Don't let me take them glasses off!' And I said I would do the mate the favor, aye."

Mike Potter, the makeup artist, had crooned through his little sharp teeth, "You tell them, Speedie." He flipped his hair out of his eyes for a second. I stood passively behind Laura like a kid at her parent's knees. As Potter motioned to me to sit in a chair so that he could apply the finishing touches to my foundation, he announced, "Speedie, you're as diva as Madonna. I am going to nickname you . . . Matuna! JT, you sit down. You, Matuna, cool it. I'll do your eyelashes later."

Through a cloud of face powder, I had glimpsed Steven, who was warmly tanned, his blond hair naturally falling behind his ears. He studiously watched Potter make me up as Jodie Foster in *Taxi Driver*. The stylist, Ariana Philips, had chosen butterfly glasses, tinsel tights, and hot shorts, which made me worry about my hips. That was where one could tell, wasn't it? One of Steven's hands was propped against his other resting halfway over his mouth. He'd asked again, "But why the glasses, JT?"

"It makes me feel uncomfortable. Takin' pictures is hard as it is," I'd stammered.

Laura jumped in, "Let alone 'avin' someone capture his eyes. Without the glasses there's no protection. Nothin' in between 'im and the world, and 'e feels like 'e's put so much out in the books, 'e can't give his whole self. Also 'e wants to 'ave the freedom to be fluid with his gender. Sometimes 'e goes out as a boy, and other days he goes out as a girl. 'E takes that freedom. It's not a game." Laura had said. "'E will not take them off."

I could understand why Steven wanted me to lose the glasses. I was stiff and deadpan as it was, and the glasses added to the formulaic quality of my poses. On the ride back from the airport, Steven had commented how difficult it had been to tease any emotion out of his underwear model. The boy had refused to look him in the eyes. Steven told me, "You want to know if the model is shy or confident or sweet or jaded. You want his outside appearance to resonate with an emotion coming from his eyes. But if he can't look you in the face, you're left with a blank slate." I nodded in agreement.

At Laura's request, Mike Potter and Holli Pops, the hair stylist, had created JT a "scab and laceration" wig. It was a scruffy ashen blond cut jaggedly with razors. Tiny ruby droplets of fake blood and sutures peeked out from bald spots. Holli was from San Francisco, too. I had met her once briefly, about a year and a half before, but she didn't seem to remember me, which was lucky, I guess. But I definitely remembered her.

Holli trimmed a fake moustache for JT. "I'm going to put this on you."

"No, no. Please," I whispered in protest, feeling flushed.

"Then I'll leave it here and let you put it on." She had set it down on the dresser indulgently.

I sneaked a few glances at her. Her eyes were glacier blue, which offset the bright fuchsia lipstick she wore.

Potter came in. "Okay, JT, go and put on your facial hair."

"Okay," I tried to say airily.

I went into the bathroom and caked the glue onto my upper lip, which reminded me of dying my own moustache when I was younger. The thought of putting it on with Holli Pops in the room made me feel self-conscious. JT was supposedly impossibly shy, and I felt as if his shyness were seeping into me, giving me permission to cave into my fears. Emerging from the bathroom, I grabbed Laura by the shoulder and whispered, "I think I like Holli."

Laura giggled conspiratorially and said, "You do?"

I didn't know what she was up to. Laura sidled up to Mike and said with a grin, "Guess who JT's got a crush on?"

"Who?" Mike asked excitedly.

"Holli!" She whispered giddily.

Potter looked at me a little confused, "You know, Holli has a brother who looks just like her."

"I didn't know that," I said barely able to look at them, wanting to scratch the moustache right off my face.

I glared at Laura, feeling powerless, buttoning up my resentment.

After a few hours Steven said, "Let's break for lunch." Laura whispered a complaint about the Subway sandwiches that Gabriel had bought to keep the three-day shoot on budget. Steven looked at the foot-longs on waxed paper, then led us quietly by our elbows out of the hotel room, motioning us to follow him down the steps and cobbled path toward dining tables outside. He stopped beside a plot of freshly bedded tulips and said, "I'm gonna treat you to lunch today."

"Oh thank you, Steven. It's just that JT gets really wiggy. I try to keep him away from corporate food. It doesn't have to be ornate, just not crap, y'know?"

The host sat us down on the patio in a yellow rose garden directly across from Leonardo DiCaprio, who did not look up from his newspaper as we arrived. The sun was hot, and I was starving. I looked down at the sparse menu. "I'm gonna have the roast beef sandwich," I said, enunciating.

"You don't eat roast beef, JT!" Laura exclaimed.

"I do today," I said defiantly.

"JT wants the roast beef, then roast beef it is!" Steven said signaling for the waiter.

Mariela patted at the wax with her manicured fingers and blew on it gently. It turned opaque and peeled at its edges as if it were a ripe scab, then she gracefully ripped. The underside revealed white pearls at the stems of the uplifted hairs. My vision blurred as she pulled, and I heard my short gusts of breath from far away, as if they weren't my own. Mariela worked methodically. She left a mound of hair on my pubic bone, low and clipped. I marveled that I could relinquish complete control to a stranger, yet I still struggled with Laura over how JT should look and behave. Every time I complained, Laura tried to make me see what I was getting out of being JT (the equivalent pay of my shifts at the Thai restaurant, beautiful clothes from the fashion shoots, fantastic dinners). She would say, "I always look at things this way: am I getting paid for this opportunity? If I am not getting paid, am I learning from it or enjoying myself? You have a combination of all three!" I would look up and pout. It had happened too fast. I hadn't realized when I first impersonated JT that I would be signing my life over to being him. Now I was trying to take it back.

Mariela lotioned and powdered my raw skin. She went over the pubic line again with fine tweezers, weeding out the surviving hairs. Finally, she slid her palms over one another, and with a light clap, exclaimed, "*Muite bon!*"

I opened my eyes. "It's done?"

As I walked out of the salon, my spine straightened and my head lifted. I felt as if the fat on my pubic bone, that fat which every woman has, was dissolving. My stomach groaned again, but I decided that I would eat later. I needed a Brazilian bikini to go with my wax.

As I walked down the long shaded avenues, I spotted a sign with an animated green bikini bottom. Inside the cool shop the ceiling fan pumped rhythmically a little off its axis. The saleswoman was about my age, tan with chestnut curls that wound around the nape of her neck.

She looked up from her crossword puzzle and said, "*Oi.*"

"*Oi,*" I replied.

The bathing suits were stretched over round metal rods like skins over drums. I went to the first rack and scanned it until I found a black bikini, with splotches of grey. I grabbed it off the rack, suddenly feeling very dizzy.

"*Mais grande?*"

She looked at me and said, in perfect English, "I think that is the only one I have. But it will fit you."

I was relieved that she spoke English, but also disappointed. I suddenly felt like a clumsy, very white American tourist. I held onto the counter.

"Why don't you try it on?"

"I'm afraid it's too small."

"You waxed?"

I nodded.

"Then there is nothing to fear. Go in there to try it on."

I kicked off my white flip-flops and wiggled out of my clothes. I slowly glanced up at myself in the mirror. I had that brittle after-flu feeling as if my body might shatter. I flexed my newly formed Capoeira muscles and weaved my legs into the skinny bottoms. It had double straps on the sides. I looked at the back, where a tiny V tucked out of the expanse of my pale behind. The floor was cool on my bare feet.

I tried to snap the bikini further over my crack. I viewed my profile and tightened my stomach.

I remembered the first day I stepped into the Brazilian Cultural Center. I had wanted to look like the bristling women who kicked and vaulted around Marcia. Capoeira sculpts each body slightly differently, but everyone ends up with broad shoulders, muscular round butts, and jutting thighs. Capoeiristas wear white, narrow polyester pants, gusseted in the crotch, which gives everyone, man or woman, a little extra bread in the basket. The group I watched held their pants up with brightly dyed cotton cords, denoting one's growth and skill. On top, they wore cotton T-shirts with the Abada logo. I'd never seen so many strong, confident, beautiful women gathered in one room. Everything about Capoeira both attracted and intimidated me. I vowed that I would learn to assert myself with kicks, protect myself with ducks and dodges, and impress others with aerials. I could hardly believe that I was here on my pilgrimage: it was the beginning, perhaps of my new life.

"So?" the sales girl called.

"I'll take it."

I walked to the beach straight down from the store, veering towards the rocks. I wore the black bikini under a woven red and orange sarong that the saleswoman had explained could be used instead of a towel. I picked a spot of sand above everyone so that I could watch people, and better regulate who watched me. That was one thing that being JT had taught me: how to watch. The beach was like a marketplace, the calls of different vendors rising and mixing together. Each vendor had a particular style to his hawking, some musical and reeling, some sneaky and almost lude. I pulled out my phrase book (inserting it inside another book so as not to advertise my naivete) to find out that they were selling green coconut, salty pastries, grilled shrimp with garlic, beer, soft drinks, and caipirinhas. They carried sunblock and coconut oil tied to broom handles, dangling like golden fruit, heaved stacks of cigarettes and tiny black cigars, lugged coolers full of popsicles and fruit cocktail with whipped cream, and waved towels emblazoned with the Brazilian flag. Against a backdrop of ocean, the silhouettes of the luxuriously oiled sunbathers vacillated in the heat. In the distance an oil rig rose and fell like an insect caught in honey. I felt beads of sweat forming on my upper lip, in my pits, and in the creases of my freshly waxed groin. Soon I would bury everything in the sand and swim.

The shrimp griller passed close in front of me wearing a dirty soccer jersey. He winked, holding his tray straight above his head. It shielded his face, and he purred something in Portuguese. I mumbled in Portuguese, "*Nao, nao. Obrigada.*"

I looked to my right to see who would be mocking me if I got up to go swimming. A young man was doing calisthenics next to the boardwalk in the shade of palms. His muscles were knotted and wiry. He must have done this routine every day. A little envious, I wondered how many reps it would take to get abs like that. And what does he think of me? I'm not his type; I'm too pale and boyish for him. I glanced left to an older woman, sun-wizened, in an orange halter bikini. She'd arranged her matching high heels beside her on her blanket, where she sat reading a pulpy magazine. I thought I knew who she was just by her coiffed hair. She had maids to make her lunch, and grown children. What does she think of me? My mind was beginning to spiral . . . What did Steven Klein think of me back at the photoshoot, with my "scab and lacerations" wig and my made-up face? He thought JT wasn't doing the look justice. The props didn't have emotion on their own. It was the wearer's job to imbue them with feeling. I wasn't doing that for him, or for JT.

I'd wanted so badly to please him during that shoot, to give him what he wanted, but I couldn't loosen up. He told me to take a five-minute break, and I wandered into the kitchen, where a few production assistants were hanging out smoking pot and drinking rum. I had a few hits, hoping that it would help. I went back out to the brightly lit living room where we were shooting and backed up against the wall, feeling like a discovered rodent, frozen and unsure which way to run. I dragged my feet along the wall. My moustache twitched. I tried to hunch into a tough pose for Steven. I was confused. What did he want? I felt myself edging away from the light with jagged steps. They are all looking at me, waiting for me to do something interesting. I began to feel more and more queasy. Before I knew what I was doing, I took a mincing step back and puked my roast beef sandwich into a wicker garbage can. I handed my moustache, soaked in vomit, to Mike Potter, and Steven clicked way, delighted to finally get some action.

It would be time to swim soon, and I was still trying to get used to the idea of having such a bare ass. As I contemplated buying a pair of shorts, a beautiful woman walked by and sat down in front of me along with an entourage of five men, whom I hoped were her brothers. She was tall with broad shoulders and narrow hips. Her hair was clipped in tight curls. She had caramel skin, amber eyes, and golden hair at the crook of her back and on her arms. A dark wiry treasure trail wound its way up her belly, which stuck out softly. She wore long beaded earrings and a lavender crocheted bikini. The idea of a swim blew away in the salty breeze. I could never show my ass in its current state to such a beautiful woman. I wrapped the red and orange sarong tightly around my waist and propped my head up on my elbow, pretending to focus on my book. To my astonishment, she glanced back at me.

The men rolled a joint. They were oiled up, galloping around her in their bold Speedos. Maybe they were performers, and she was the master of ceremonies? An itinerant bartender passed by with a styrofoam cooler, calling out "*Skol-a-skol-a-skol.*" The group bought beers all around. One of them rubbed his chest with a frosty can. Perhaps that was her boyfriend? She popped her beer, then turned her head slightly and again, to my utter disbelief, she raised her can to me. How should I respond? I sat up, trying to look natural. She glanced back again. She was subtle, barely turning her head. I thought to myself, this is what it's all about. I came here, to Rio, for this moment. I decided to take a swim. I stood up, making sure I didn't let my hand go for my wedgie. I stretched and started to take assured long strides past her and her brothers. They nodded slightly as I passed. I walked into the water without hesitation. I gripped my feet into the shifting sand, letting the icy water envelop me. I dove in, feeling the waves pulling at each other. As I came up again, I felt cleansed. I swam past the breakers, letting my head bob up and down. Finally, I paddled back in, shaking a little.

My body went slightly numb. I felt transformed. I walked past the woman again. She smiled.

Suddenly, someone on the boardwalk whistled at my backside. Another asshole, I thought. The beautiful woman glanced back. He whistled again. I couldn't help it; I reluctantly turned, too. He was a powerfully built black man with dreadlocks. He wore tight jean shorts and a fanny pack; his legs were thick as tree trunks. He smiled, his eyes glowing intensely with sex. I turned my head and pretended as if I hadn't noticed him.

"*Oi*," he had a scratchy voice, and he said in stilted English, "Little One, I picked you out because of your white skin."

I thought, can't you see I'm busy? Fuck off.

He went on, "*Eu sou Capoeirista.*"

I recognized that word. I was still mistrustful but dropped my guard slightly.

"I am not from here, either," he said.

Like I care, I thought.

He continued, "I am from the South, de Grupo Abada."

That was the group I was meant to meet up with! I looked at the white fabric he cradled in his arms. It was a pair of our pants, the logo Abada embroidered on it. Incredible.

I asked, "Do you know Marcia Cigarra?"

"Marcia! The Cicada? Marcia is one of my sisters!"

"I'm her student," I said, not quite believing the way things happen sometimes.

"No! *Qual serendipidade!* You come for the games? From Sao Francisco?"

I nodded.

"My name is Gororoba. I am going to teach a class tonight as a guest. All the Americans who stay at the Hostel Internationale will be there. Allow me to introduce one of my students, Batatina." If I'm not mistaken, his name means "little potato."

A man-cub, about seventeen, came shuffling from the boardwalk, kneeled and extended a paw toward me, "Batatina, *plasir*."

By this time the beautiful woman and her brothers had smoked their joints and crushed their beer cans. They were dusting the sand off of their behinds and stretching. She glanced back at me and nodded one last time; one of her brothers gave me a thumbs-up. Suddenly, one of her entourage threw a beer can at her feet. She broke out in full grin and lunged for his ankles. She grappled him down and mock kicked him. When finished, she put her hands on her hips. She gave Gororoba and me a quick playful smile then turned. I marveled at the confidence in her eyes.

ROME

IN THE CUSTOMS LINE at the Rome airport, I bent over our bags and ripped off the tags. "Should we replace them with JT's name?" I was hush so that the people waiting in front of us wouldn't wonder what was going on. Laura said, "Good idea, we'll do it next time," as she lathered sunscreen on her nose and cheeks.

Within a week of our American–European book tour, we settled into our roles as big and little sister. Our schedule was packed with events: readings, book signings, photo shoots, and dinners with people JT had become close friends with over the telephone and through email. A few days into the New York leg I had my first live interview. I had flailed during each question, while Laura, ever the "handler" as she had been nicknamed, charged to fill in the answers, prefacing them with "JT once told me . . ."

After doing a photo shoot with Mick Rock, we went back to our hotel room. I was flossing my teeth as Laura shaved her legs. I realized that we had reached some intimacy and new understanding of each other. I slipped on a plaid nightgown and sat down on the tiled floor. Laura put on pajama bottoms and a T-shirt with the *Harold's End* logo from the Los Angeles reading. She always wore T-shirts with quirky sayings like, "Fame is not sexually transmitted." She slid down onto the tiles next to me and said, "This is like an arranged marriage, where the couple really falls in love. You are so perfect for this. And I can see you blossoming and growing into yourself. You have such a sense of self already." She traced the lines of grout where they intersected.

"No, I don't," I contested.

I thought back on the day. We met Mick Rock in the Chelsea Hotel. He had sat me on a giant gold-leafed hand in front of a large speckled canvas. The stylist had bound my eyes and hands with fuchsia-silk netting. I watched Mick through a hot-pink web, as he squinted through his shaded glasses. He popped two tablets of Vitamin C, mixing them with a bit of water on his tongue and letting them bubble. Taking off his jean jacket and throwing it on a chair, he did a few whirls bent over, stretching out on his back. Mike Potter came over and sat down on his knees, arranging a row of bottles and brushes. He embossed the words "virtue" and "sin" on my hands. He then dusted my cheeks with rose blush, pulling my long blond wig to one side of my head.

Mick took a Polaroid. Pulling up the strip of fabric from my eyes, he showed me the proofs, saying in his British accent, "There's contradiction here—it's a fantastic image." I looked down, feeling self-conscious that my thighs looked too big in my khaki pants. Mick roared, "Let out your discomfort, JT! Do what you need to do here! Scream! Release it!" We put the eye-patch back on. I opened my mouth, and adjusting my voice to a lower octave, I began to growl like I was gargling with salt.

"That's it! Let it go, JT, whatever it is! Reclaim yourself!"

Raising my voice, I searched for a more comfortable pitch, trying to prolong the sound. My voice cracked and my heart beat with a thud in my ears. I hit some stride, finding myself screaming incredibly loud. I thought, I must be breaking through something. At least a few blood vessels.

Stopping and wiping his forehead with a handkerchief, Mick knelt over the chair, showing me a Polaroid of these shots. He had taken it through a fish-eye lens from above. My hands were pulled taut. "I think we've got something," he said.

"When I was young I had no idea who I was." Laura tugged on her crocheted hat, and continued. "There were points when I was so aimless, when I thought I'd just kill myself. But when I look back on all that has led up to now, there was always an inkling of my truths. And there was always something leading me to this place. It was like a tree branch I would follow, and the leaves and fruit grew around me. Life felt stark and brittle when I took a wrong turn, like the branch would break underneath me. And my out was always suicide. Now I feel us blossoming. We are on the right path. Don't you think?"

I didn't know. I said flatly, "I don't feel like any of it has much to do with me." And wondered to myself, why was I doing it then?

"It has a lot to do with you. People are responding to you. They can't not. This *is* you." Laura traced one whole tile with her finger. "No matter what soil you throw on top of it or how you dress it up, it's you. They are responding to you."

"It doesn't feel that way," I mumbled.

We feasted on our leftover meals of grilled polenta and chicken that we had eaten earlier. We stretched out on the floor and crossed our legs. It was like laying a lunch down by our own private river, no one around but us. Every night Laura told me stories about growing up. She gave me every detail, down to what she was made to wear as a child. With each recounting, parts of her personality came flying into place. That night she told me about Sarah, whose family had invented the bottle cap. Sarah, who was the inspiration for JT's mother. As she told me about her childhood friend, she seemed to go into a trance. And when she felt me nodding off, she painted my face like she did with Thor—my eyelids, my cheeks—in loose round strokes, telling me what colors she was using as she went.

As I stooped to undo the last of the tags, I could smell her green-tea sunblock mixing with frankincense, which she always applied, behind her ears, in her cleavage, and if we were in an opportune place, down her tights, which she always wore except to bed. I was wearing my wig and sunglasses. We moved outside of the line. "We're in no hurry to go through customs. That line will be there when JT is ready to go through those doors." Laura had no problem separating herself from the herd.

Before the trip, Laura had been in and out of the hospital for her calcium levels, so she had acquired official wheelchair privileges at the airport. We cut through the sprawling line with people glaring at us.

We always had too much carry-on luggage—at least two

small pieces of luggage filled with our clothing, a backpack full of Laura's vitamins, makeup, and dental care supplies (she never went anywhere without her electric toothbrush), and a big paper bag full of treats and bottles of water. With wheelchair privileges we could pile everything onto her lap. A man would get us through to our gate. Laura always generously tipped the people who pushed her the extra distance.

When we got out of the airplane in Rome, Laura didn't bother calling for the wheelchair. As we exited, the beige doors swung open onto a crowd of families and limousine drivers holding up placards. I spotted the four employees of our Italian publisher Fazi, with a sign scrawled in a thick marker: "JT!!!"

Simone, who was about five-foot-four with a receding hairline and eyeglasses that seemed to fog up from his smile, held the sign. He shouted in a thick accent "JT!" He stood there with Loretta, a tall woman with an elegant bob, and Valeria, who was younger with long curly brown hair and ripped jeans.*

Laura asked to sit in the front seat of the car because of "me long legs." Simone packed our three huge bags into the trunk of the roller skate-sized car but had to fit the third on Valeria's lap. He got in the driver's seat and flipped on *Generation X*, turning back to me to say, "JT! I know you like it. Billy Idol's debut!" I noticed his chest build and collapse as he spoke.

Both of the women looked over at me. It took me a second and I replied, "Yeah. I love it. How did you know?"

---

* I may be misremembering some of the names of my Italian publishers.

Simone took his hand off the wheel as if he was demonstrating the horizon, pointing at the tenements and green fields and cocked his head, "I just know."

Laura said, "Yeah, we listen to this stuff all the time at home with our boy. I grew up on this stuff!"

Simone looked over to her, his forearms leaning on the wheel now, looking straight at her. "Oh yes? And where did you grow up, Speedie?" I knew his driving was irritating her. She couldn't stand it when people took their eyes off the road. I could tell she was debating whether to tell him.

"All over. Eyes on the road, now! Me pa was a man of the government, but I ran away and lived in squats starting when I was a green bean. This was the hot album back then. JT just found out about a lot of this music. Right, JT? You grew up with some of it 'cause of your ma. Keep your eyes on the road now, look alive!" He didn't seem to hear her.

I nodded vigorously.

"At home he doesn't go out at all. You should consider yourselves blessed."

"Oh, we do!" Simone exclaimed. "It is an honor, JT. An honor. We really love your work! We were not sure if you would come or not. We are very excited." He turned down the music. "So, now we have espresso and snack. And then we drop you off for a shower, and we meet you at the press conference. Asia, she come to pick you up in a taxi at your hotel with Loretta." I looked over and she smiled. He continued, "Then lunch with Fazi himself, and his son. He comes just to meet you. I think you will like him. And tomorrow you and Asia will read in the Siepe at night for the literature festival." By now I was having mini heart attacks. A press conference? A reading? Holy fuck. Right off the plane? I needed to cram to prepare myself. Simone must have noticed my electric socket response because he said, "Don't worry, JT. We going to draw you up an itinerary."

Laura said, "Yeah, we need that. Otherwise we'll never remember any of this. Fazi knows how to put the boy to work, eh?"

"Well, it's busy now because of the festival, but later we will have time for sight-seeing."

Valeria added, "And we will see Garbage perform later in the trip. I like that song they made for you, JT. It's very good!"

I wished they would just be quiet for a second so I could focus on my hysteria.

Laura began to sing, "'Go on boy, go.' Yeah, that song has reached the charts. We get amazing reactions to the books. Bono was quoted saying the book is blowing his mind, and Madonna just read it . . ."

She went on and on, and they all listened with rapt attention, exclaiming with delight as she reeled through the list of accolades from famous fans.

Laura had given me a bunch of print interviews with JT to look at on the plane, but I only read a few, then fell asleep. Laura had also given me an article about Asia. I had never heard of her. It was in *I-D* magazine, a spaciously laid out, lap-sized magazine with grainy black and white portraits of Asia, pregnant, smoking in the bathtub. I got the feeling she loved to shock people. JT and Asia had been emailing for a few months. Laura implied their exchanges were flirtatious.

We had packed a chicken for the airplane ride. Pointing with her drumstick, Laura said, "I have a good feeling about her." I had already popped a sleeping pill, having eaten my share of the chicken.

"Love me some chicken!" Then Laura popped an Ambien, too.

As it set in, we looked at each other cross-eyed and began giggling.

The magazines that Laura wrote for seemed like a road map of pop culture—lacquered portraits, fashion spreads, and articles written by people who had their fingers on the pulse of everything important. I wallowed in the fashion spreads. They've already done that? I fretted, biting my nails. I was going to do that in duct tape! My passion for clothing was piqued by designers' interest in JT. I was on my way to collecting a trove of unisex clothes. Calvin Klein offered to custom-make JT a suit, and he gave me a slew of beautifully tailored pants. I had never gotten my hands on beautiful clothes like these, and I was amazed at how empowered the well-tailored clothing made me feel. My means had so far been limited, but I was inspired to go beyond duct tape.

"We're going to eat breakfast, right?" Laura directed this question to Simone. "Because JT can't do a bunch of press without eating something." The last thing I needed was food. I glared at her.

"We go to get a snack now."

"But will there be eggs and stuff like that?"

"Ah, I don't know, we will see. It will be good. You don't have to worry, Speedie."

"That's my job, Simone. They don't call me JT's handler for nothing."

We arrived at what looked like a bakery. The waiter brought us into a vaulted, many-mirrored room. He started filling the table with silver-tiered trays of pastries and colorful cookies. Everyone ordered espresso so I ordered espresso too, and Laura asked, "A mochachino? Or macchiato? Can they put chocolate in it?" I slammed my espresso and ordered another. They passed around blond cookies, cookies with jam, and chocolate spread, but I refused each one. I could feel the caffeine setting in. I was worried about gaining weight with the way Laura and I had been eating, especially late at night. In reaction, I was on a special regiment during the days. Coffee and red ginseng until I couldn't speak: that was how I knew I was ready to begin eating. I resented Laura's obsession with food, feeling that just when I was about able to practice self-control, she threw me back into my own dysfunctions.

After coffee, I felt more hysterical and less tired. While nobody was looking I popped a beaker of ginseng for good measure. The plan was that Loretta would wait in the lobby as we changed our clothes at the hotel. Asia would come shortly after.

Our dim hotel lobby felt like the living room of a great aunt who loves cats and never leaves the house. The concierge looked at us with disdain. He dragged our bags through the narrow stairwell to our room, which was musty. It consisted of a queen-sized bed and a vanity.

"You want to take a shower? We have a little time," Laura said in a gentle way, then mumbled, "Guess Fazi hasn't made it big yet. Lucky they got JT on their team."

As I undressed, her tone changed. "I knew it. I knew they would do that. I need eggs in the morning. You know how you need coffee? I need eggs. None of this sugar breakfast. I get loopy." I jumped in the shower, turning the cold faucet. It was humid here. I left the door open. It was a claw foot tub with an opaque shower curtain. The vines at the window blurred green. Was she blaming me for the cookie breakfast?

"I need you to be my advocate in the future. People don't listen to what I need, so I need you to speak up for me." That was true. People didn't respond to her demands in the same way that they responded to JT's. In fact, they were often hostile to them. I am not taking care of Laura's needs, I thought guiltily. But I was also starting to resent this fucked-up dynamic. Why was she always dependent on others to get what she needed?

"I get it." Rolling my eyes, I let the cold water run over my head. I wasn't going to get into it with her this time. We had already had many versions of this conversation on other JT outings. I would bellow, "Why should I order something I don't want to eat?"

"Why do you only think of yourself? Maybe someone else would want to eat it. Like your brother, or your nephew. You can always pack it up." Frustrated, she would often say, "You're such a goy!" She'd point out that my people had never suffered through the years, so we never felt the need to take extra for loved ones. In fact, I'd had the opposite training. My parents both had an aversion to excess. They never bought paper towels. My father left everything dirty, and my mother compulsively washed everything with old dishrags worn threadbare; then she compulsively washed those. On Saturdays, Hennessey and I got on our hands and knees and dusted underneath the beds and bathtub with these rags. My mother wore her clothes until they were full of holes, elbows worn out like someone's jaws hanging open. She only bought enough groceries for one day at a time. And when people came over for dinner they went home and ate again because the portions were so small at our house.

My father was frugal in a different way. He never threw anything away. He refused to pay full price for his produce, so he would scout out "perfectly good" tomatoes and apples in the bruise bin of the discount food store and buy them in bulk. He kept every plastic bag to pack up bruised fruit or to use as garbage bags. On a recent camping trip, when we cooked a meal together, he pointed out, "You missed a spot!" There was a little grain sticking to the lip of the pot that I accordingly scraped into the serving bowl. I had never realized where I inherited this part of my own meagerness until that moment.

Laura is clean, much cleaner than I am, but as soon as she enters a room she messes it up. She could do it in a matter of minutes, flooding the space with magazine articles, loose pieces of paper, plastic bags, and chocolate wrappers. As soon as she went into a bathroom she would throw the fluffy white hotel towels onto the floors. She hated how the cold tile felt on her bare feet. This habit bothered me. I hated the feeling of wrinkled fabric under my feet.

Laura was always on the hunt. She would carry plastic zip lock bags to take extra food from a buffet, and shopping bags for "other things." You never knew what you might come upon. She would pat herself on the back afterwards for her resourcefulness, committed to whatever she had foraged. She would disperse things to others even if they didn't want her free shit. I think they would take it out of politeness. Sometimes there was someone who genuinely appreciated that stolen toilet paper or pound of year-old peanut brittle. Nothing seemed to please Laura as much as this. But to me, it was excess. It exhausted me because I was trying to find a place for it to go. I could relate to foraging, and it wasn't that I didn't like free things. But quantity freaked me out.

"What if I don't know the answers?" I said, changing my tone to a whine. I had only done that one interview in New York and it hadn't gone very well. This time Laura wouldn't be there to back me up. My stomach felt cramped from anxiety about the upcoming press, and distended and heavy from traveling.

I got out of the shower and frisked myself dry, wrapping the towel around me. I pulled out Laura's past interviews. There were so many questions about JT's life. Why didn't they ask about his writing? Reporters rarely asked about the books, more mesmerized by his survivor story. As long as people stuck to questions about the mundane details of JT's life, I was okay. What was JT's favorite color? Yellow. His taste in literature? Nabokov, Flannery O'Connor, Breece D'J Pancake. He liked Wiffle ball and dark chocolate. We definitely didn't have the same taste in music; he had Laura's taste. It shouldn't have mattered to me, but I am a music snob. And it pained me to say I liked Pearl Jam and Silverchair. And it seemed to hint that JT was not who he said he was. None of my peers—JT and I were supposed to be the same age—liked the new music Laura listened to.

At the readings in New York and Los Angeles, I met fans who were hungry for JT's acknowledgment. They told me how the books had affected them, and they recounted their own life stories. I listened silently and held their hands. I rationalized to myself that JT was a conduit for many people who had suffered and survived. JT existed as a force of energy flying above our heads, a symbol of hope for those who had undergone the same kind of trauma and lived through it. Laura, JT, and I were a trinity. I didn't know what our mission was yet, but I knew it was something bigger than our trivial problems and rivalries.

Loretta brusquely rapped on the wooden door. "Asia is downstairs." I dropped my dirty underwear on the floor. "Shit, that was quick!"

Laura went to the door, "Right, hold on! JT's just getting dressed. We'll be down in two shakes!" She turned back, directing her head to the door. "If he ever finds his underwear!" she added as I riffled through a pile of dirty clothes that had exploded from my bag. I primped my wig on my hand like I had seen Mike Potter do.

I scrambled to put on the same clothes, and a new undershirt. We had gotten my pants from a designer named Gary Graham, whom we met through Mike Potter. They were made out of hand-dyed canvas, an almost metallic brown, with channels of cording around the knees. Then I put on an old white synthetic lace shirt from the '60s that I had stolen from the costume room at boarding school, an old man's v-neck, and a bomber that I had gotten from a stylist, with a cracked white leather arrow coming up and around the shoulder. I furrowed my brow as I zipped up my bomber.

"Don't worry! Don't take it so seriously! At play in the fields of the Lord!" said Laura.

When did JT split with his mother? How did he get to San Francisco? A ship bottoms-up flashed before my eyes. My veneer would slowly crumble. Laura pushed a penis bone into my hand and said, "Here, this is for her."

I could see Asia from the top of the stairs, her body swallowed up by a velvet chair. Smoke curled up from the place where her head was. She was bouncing one knee off of the other. Her fluorescent pink fuzzy purse was like a nuclear poodle at her side. Her hand holding the armchair had many rings on it. She wore a witch's pentagram. Loretta sat on a chaise, her legs crossed primly. She saw us right away and clapped her hands together, exclaiming, "Here he is!" I kept my head down low.

Asia leaned over the arm of the chair; her eyelashes drooped over her eyes, but she had an expectant pose, like a child awaiting a present. "JT!"

I barely moved my head, keeping my shoulders scrunched up. "You are that shy?" She changed her demeanor. "You are like a nut: you need to be cracked open. What is this? You act as if you don't even know me after all of our back and forth." She hadn't looked at Laura standing behind me. I should respond more, I thought. I turned my fist over and opened my hand like the maw of a snake. She took it, her eyes still on me.

"He has been looking forward to seeing you." Laura explained, and then Asia looked at her without any acknowledgment that she was JT's friend.

Loretta added, "This is JT's dear friend, Speedie."

"Right." She stared at me with her arms straight against her armchair. I kept my head down but wanted to look at her. I could feel my body shaking like a little dog. Her arms were lithe and muscular.

Loretta said, "We should go. We don't want to be late. I am going to call a taxi."

She walked out briskly, her high heels clicking down the stairs.

I ventured, "It's good to finally meet you."

Asia continued to stare at me. It felt like someone sticking their elbow into my ribs. Her look said, who the fuck are you?

"I'm sorry, I'm really nervous. I've been waiting for months to meet you, and now . . ." I trailed off.

Where was this bullshit spewing from? My body felt incredibly tense, as if I had been contracting my muscles for many minutes. Loretta called for us. The taxi was waiting. Laura and I labored down the stairs; we were carrying two large shopping bags full of penis bones and books and hollow chocolate trolley trains to pass out as gifts. I sat in the middle, between Laura and Asia. Laura pulled out the jars of jam and JT's two books in English.

"He said he'd sign these for you later . . ."

Asia didn't move her head.

"So how was it working on *XXX*?" Laura asked.

Asia jutted out her lip.

"It was . . . Well, what do you think?"

"I don't know. I mean, it's such a big-budget film, it seems like it would be fun in certain respects." I could feel Laura searching for something, anything she could say to connect with Asia.

"No, it was very flat. As flat as the movie was, that's how it was working on it. It was just to pay the bills."

I watched the view pass by in a blur, unsure of what to say to hold Asia's attention, content to let Laura struggle to figure it out. I was certain that she would.

"You have a child, right?" That was a winning topic of conversation for most parents.

"Yes." Asia growled. "Ana Lou. She is one-and-a-half years old."

"Astor and I've got a son together. He'll be five."

"Yeah, JT told me."

"It's been really strange to have to be so responsible all the time. You know, to have to get up at a certain time and make food at a certain time. We had been floating for so long . . . JT really cleaned up when Thor came around, though. He's even stopped swearing so much, which is one of my big issues. He's got a mouth like a sailor."

We arrived at a tall gated door of oxidized metal, which opened to a dark hallway.

"Have you been here?" I whispered to Asia.

"Never."

I noticed that Asia had a great walk, as if she were putting out cigarette butts with each step. She was elusive and hot. Loretta brought us out to a courtyard full of wooden folding chairs. Under the canopy I heard the clatter of sophisticated small talk. The courtyard was laid with old bricks overgrown with weeds. At the front there was a podium with a microphone. That was where I would hide. Reporters immediately started to snap photos of us.

Loretta dragged me to the podium. I could hear everyone getting into their seats. There were red glowing blind spots burned into my retinas. I could barely see Asia and Laura settled into two seats in the front row. Loretta tapped at the microphone and started to introduce me in Italian. I was shaking, and every so often I would jerk my head, like I was trying to pull a crick out of my neck. Someone gently placed a cup of sparkling water on the podium. I grabbed it, my hand shaking, and downed it. My head jerked again. I listened to Loretta's round vowels reverberating off the microphone. There was a quiet clicking.

She said something and everyone laughed wryly. I could tell she was wrapping it up now. "I present JT." They clapped. Laura gestured to me to say something. She looked pleased. I felt jealous that she and Asia were sitting together while I was up there awaiting my demise. I mustered a low, "Hi." Someone coughed. What were they waiting for? Were they second-guessing me? People began to raise their hands.

Loretta pointed at them. She had hands like a bird. She seemed to know all of them.

"Yes, Antonia."

Antonia shot off a question.

Loretta nodded her head.

She said, "Ah, they want to know, what are the wig and glasses for?"

I was relieved that we had started with something easy.

"Um," I breathed heavily into the microphone, "I put so much into the books. I wear the wig so that people won't recognize me, so that I can keep something for me that's personal. Same thing with my eyes." I pushed a last breath into the microphone. The sun spots were receding.

In practically all the interviews, this question came up in one form or another. The most direct had been in another city, when an interviewer said, "You could be anybody. How do we know you are who you say you are? I mean, you sound like a woman to me." The rest of the reporters muttered and shook their head at him, indignant that he had asked such a question. They considered him a nut. I would be saved each time by remembering Laura's "Chinese Finger Puzzle" rule: always go in further to get out.

"Um, you don't know. And you won't know. And I don't want you to know. JT could be back in Spokane, a 500-pound black man, like that guy, the voice of Elmo, right? Some people say I am Dennis Cooper. Some people say I am really Gus Van Sant. I like that. I mean, yer absolutely right. I could be anybody. As fer sounding like a woman, thank you." I curtsied.

"These stories are so personal, why did you write them?"

I explained how JT frequently called Dr. Terrence Owens, the head of the children's ward, and how he encouraged JT to write. "The stories were written as therapy." That seemed to cap it.

In my head I thought, this is what I had always tried to create as a kid: an interactive imaginary world. I was reminded of all of the games I played as a child, pretending

Savannah playing
dress-up at age four.

Savannah and Hilo, 2000.

Laura, Geoff, and Savannah in photo booth strips, 2002.

Savannah, as JT LeRoy posing as a boy, 2001. COURTESY OF MARY ELLEN MARK

Savannah and Asia Argento, on the beach, 2002. COURTESY OF JUERGEN TELLER

JT, "letting it go," in the studio with Mick Rock, 2002.

Savannah and Asia, 2002.

Backstage at the Public Theater for an *Index Magazine* Evening with JT Leroy and Friends, 2003. Including Tatum O'Neil, Laura Albert, Rosario Dawson, Asia Argento, Winona Ryder, Debbie Harry, and Shirley Manson. © MICK ROCK 2008. WWW.MICKROCK.COM

Laura, Geoff, and Savannah as Speedie, Astor, and JT LeRoy, 2004. COURTESY OF SHARON HENNESSEY

Tinc's first fashion shoot, 2005. COURTESY OF SHARON HENNESSEY

to be blind, asking for money to use the payphone with a bad French accent, having fake fights with my best friends to get people to slow down in their cars.

"I've read interviews in which you have defended your mother and say that you love her. Most people reading *The Heart* would wonder, how could you have any positive feelings for her?"

Back at the hotel I had just read an interview with JT in which someone asked a question like this one. Someone coughed.

"I think Sarah tried to be a good mother. She was just too young and, um, fucked up, overwhelmed. She is just too scarred." A flop answer. Laura had said it so well. JT usually seemed so smart and clever, but today he was a bumbling idiot.

"You wrote on your website that writing is your lifesaver. Is it still true? Is it your *raison d'être?*

My *raison d'être*, I thought bitterly, is to put on a wig and speak in a lousy Southern accent.

"Uh, yeah. I think it is the same today . . ." It felt like they were waiting for something else. "Um, but I really hate writing . . . I mean, it takes me all day to sit down and write. I avoid it at all costs. It's a masochistic process." They snickered at the word.

"In your novel, Sarah says, 'We all need someone to know who we really are.' Today, do you know who you are?"

"Um, no. No, I don't think I do."

After it was over, the reporters took a flurry of pictures, and I realized that the sunspots were actually from flashbulbs.

Loretta led me off the podium. I stubbed my sneakers on the bricks and stumbled off. Laura and Asia began to clap and whoop loudly. It seemed like they were bonding. The reporters looked over at them, mildly amused, Asia skipping and pushing me from behind, and Laura kissing my head, and spitting over the wig, "Fucking brilliant!" Simone came up and said, "JT, you did great!" He introduced me to Elidor Fazi, who thumped me on the back as if I had cherry pits stuck in my throat. He was a giant man with grey hair. "You did great, JT. I thought you were going to drop your glass of water or cry, but you didn't." Loretta held me by the shoulders for a second, "Now it is the best part of the day in Italy, lunch time. You must be hungry, JT. You worked very hard." This lucky boy, I thought to myself. Everyone gives him so much encouragement. JT had earned his lunch. Good JT.

Still on tour a month later, I heard through the door, as if through a tunnel, Laura speaking on the phone. She was doing an interview. I sat in the bathtub pulling the curved handle of a long spigot and letting the hot water run pure. All through the book tour my solace had been the bathtub. This would be my last bath because we were about to go back home. We had stayed in Italy for three weeks. Asia had driven us to Milan for a reading and a press conference. The way the bookstore was set up, everyone was practically in JT's face. I whispered, "They're too close." Laura suggested doing the reading under the table, and the idea appealed to me, so I did it. It pissed off the reporters and they asked me all kinds of nasty questions afterwards.

Asia and Laura became livid, screaming together, "You know what? Fuck you!"

The next day we picked up Asia's daughter who was staying with the family of her ex. Ana Lou had big blue eyes and curly hair, and barely spoke more than a few words. Asia decided that we should stop for the night at her grandparents' house in Tuscany. Before we began driving up the hill we stopped in a cobble stone village. We bought simple supplies for the night from a little old lady. For dinner we got fresh pasta, a hard cheese, paté, basil, tomatoes, and yellow watermelon and cherries for dessert. We gathered milk, eggs, and fresh bread for the morning.

As we began to drive up the hill we could see the valley, half of it bathed in afternoon light, half of it already in darkness. The hills were covered in golden grass. The valley below was a grid of farmland and grape vines. We rolled up a dirt driveway. The house was empty. It was a beautiful old wood and earthen tile villa from the time of the Medici, Asia told us. We hurriedly put our bags down to enjoy the last of the sun. Ana Lou began to trot around in her dress, excited to run through the tall grass. We got a throw from inside and sat down on it. Asia and I made daisy chains, joining the two halves of a crown to put on Ana Lou's head. Laura cooed to Ana Lou, who took off her daisy chain and put it on Laura's head.

Despite the warmth of the sunlight a chill from the shadows of the hill began to creep into our bones. We went inside. Rifling through the cupboards, Asia found and gave to me a pair of leather britches, a snakeskin Gucci belt, and a black gaucho hat that would become JT's signature. She also gave me her grandmother's psychedelic butterfly bikini, modest-cut drawers and a thick bra, which, when I lifted them up, leaked sand from the crotch like an hourglass.

After this time in Italy, Laura and I went to Sweden for three days, Amsterdam for two days, and then France, where we caught the Chunnel to England.

My limbs floated ghost-like along the incline of the porcelain tub. I felt the hot water mingling with the tepid bath. I could tell by the transition in Laura's voice that she had gotten to a certain point with the reporter. Throughout the trip, I had taken notes on important aspects of the interviews—phrasings, and certain intonations.

I heard the reporter ask something over the speaker. Laura paused, then began to answer, which she punctuated with many "ums." He had asked JT about his obsession with his mother. I could hear her say through the door that every writer is a chef with his own signature flavor. "My writing is filtered through me, so my issues are constantly there, like my shadow." Laura often spoke in metaphors. And as metaphors, what she said about JT rang true for her life as well. Sometimes I felt she went overboard in public, like she was showing off, like she was really saying, "*I'm* the writer. *I'm* the genius." She couldn't stop herself, even when we were in public and she was meant to be Speedie. I would think to myself, why is she constantly threatening to blow our cover? Who is she trying to impress? I began keeping a journal to feel more like a writer.

In Italy we had become so adroit we could tag-team the

press. I would be downstairs doing interviews in person, while she would be upstairs doing interviews for press in Britain, France and Switzerland. When I would begin speaking in JT's voice, my nose filled up with snot and my jaw worked back and forth like a guppy. The answers came out crumpled and jagged, full of stammering, "just just just" and "it it it." I would get myself into such a state of anxiety that I puked a few times, just as JT was supposed to, and if I had to get up in front of people, I would often to cry. When I would enter the room while Laura was doing an interview, I would see her pacing with the phone hooked up to her ear, or sitting on the edge of the bed rolling chocolate on her tongue, a pot of green tea next to the bedside, soymilk at the ready.

The Italian press had called JT a glutton because he spoke so obsessively about chocolate. The chocolate Laura collected from fans in Italy lasted her at least until we got to France. As I entered the room she would beckon me with her long fingers, sometimes telling the reporter, "Hold on, Speedie just walked in. Hi, Speedie!" After a few minutes I would yammer out, "Hclloo!" All high and wispy the way I had heard her do. Or she would do it, holding the phone at a distance.

I looked down at my breasts in the bathtub. I had begun to regard them as if they were a protruding extension, not a part of me, like fungi clinging to a tree. I had already been in the bath for over half an hour, and I would make a point of staying another half an hour. We had gotten into a fight, so I was not anxious to open the door.

At this point in the tour I felt like a sailor in the hull

on his twentieth week at sea, with nothing but crackers to eat and no contact with the outside world. I squinted in the steam. I had a horrible hangover. We had gone out with Juergen Teller, the photographer, whom we had met in Italy with Asia. He had taken photos of Asia draped over her black convertible with a rose in her hand. I think they were vaguely in love with one another but I wasn't jealous. I think I didn't feel threatened by him because he was older. He was a man, not a silly boy. And though he had sort of Germanic good looks—high cheek bones, blue eyes, and blond hair—his hair flopped in his face, and he had a little bit of a belly. He wasn't searching for that perfect, sleek veneer. He seemed to thrive on social dynamics. I enjoyed sitting next to him at a bar or rooftop garden, usually smoking, and watching people interact. That's what seemed to interest him most. He was a voyeur, much like Laura and me.

Juergen came out to do a photo-shoot of Asia and me, and we kept putting it off. Finally he decided we should do a shoot on the beach, so we drove there in a two-car caravan. Laura told me to have a good time; she said she didn't need to go out with us. I think she had had enough of our smoking and drinking.

The beach had a few rusted edifices painted in fading pastels. The parking lot was empty. First we had shrimp and calamari and beer in an open-air restaurant. Asia complained to the waiter that there was sand on the plates. We smoked cigarettes and put our feet up on the rickety chairs surrounding us. She had lent me her red Brazilian bathing suit, which she had gotten on the set of a movie. It had a built in wonder bra. I wondered if they would know when they saw my body that I'm a girl. I couldn't hide my hips. She squealed when I came out with the bikini on. What did that mean? She had another red bikini for herself. We lay around on lawn chairs. There I was, just one of the guys, in my red bikini. A woman came by with a basket, offering massages. Asia got one, grimacing at the pain as the woman chopped at her shoulders. It was the first time that I noticed her feet. They had tall arches, and an eyeball was tattooed on one ankle. We all went swimming, then I quickly put my clothes back on.

In London we went to Juergen's house, where we met his family, and Alice Fisher, a reporter who had been very close to JT over the years through email. I don't remember where or what we ate, which means I was already drunk. We went out after dinner without his wife to a bar in a lonely corner of town. As we walked in I noticed we were the only ones there. The bar had once been Jimi Hendrix's recording studio. Juergen announced that they had absinthe, which I had never had before. Laura put her arm around a bench, bored by the idea of more drinking. She and Alice spoke quietly. I could tell Laura wished we weren't here. The absinthe came in little shots, glowing like Kryptonite. The bartender brought them over with wet sugar cubes balanced on silver spoons. She lit a match and inflamed each cube. They glowed dull blue and yellow, which reflected onto our faces. Then she put them out with a glass pitcher of water. She brought Laura a Shirley Temple. I imagined myself as Rose Sélavy, sitting with

Man Ray. We clanged our thimbles together and drank. The owner brought out a dress that someone famous had worn; he wanted to impress us. It was pink tulle, like a Cinderella dress. I jumped up. "Let me try it on!" I had lost weight on the trip, and it looked like it would fit me. The owner brought me into the basement. There was graffiti on the walls, and he pointed out Jimi's handwriting. He said, "I'll wait outside." I felt very special. The zipper was tinny and fragile, and I couldn't get it up all the way. I bumped the door open not caring if he saw my ace bandages; they matched the color of the dress. I ran up the stairs and he came up slowly after me. There was a reggae song on that I liked, and I hummed along. Everyone exclaimed when they saw me. I started dancing around. Juergen said, "I wish I had my camera." I said, "Let's do another shot!"

They all looked at each other for a second. "Alright," Juergen said hesitantly, without the fervor that I had hoped for from my drinking partner. Laura looked at him, appalled.

"No," she said. "We have to leave tomorrow. And you have had enough."

I turned on her. "Every step I make is not directed by you, harpy! Let's do another shot!" Beginning to dance around again I spat, for emphasis, "Fuck you!" I was invincible. She wasn't going to tell me what to do.

Laura had fire coming out of her eyes. "I guess JT's a grown man. We'll do one more round," Juergen said. Laura looked at everyone at the table. "No, he's not. Look at him!" I stopped dancing. Laura's eyes landed on Alice, like she was waiting for her to say something. Alice sat there quietly, staring at me. I looked back at them; they all looked so uptight and unhappy. I went up to the bar. Laura demanded, "Do not give him that shot!" The bartender prepared me one more. I downed it quickly as she said this, simultaneously realizing my buzz was gone. Now it was more a matter of principle.

Laura stood up and left.

Everyone else stood up sheepishly. I guess it was time to go. I had forgotten that I wasn't wearing my own clothes.

I stormed off, down to the basement where I had left my clothes in a heap, settling deep into the second shot of absinthe. I hated her, I thought to myself hazily. She was a pushy, bossy, self-serving bully. I pulled my pants back on and zipped my blazer up to the neck. A crazy fucking bitch.

Earlier in the day Laura had called Asia. I was jealous of her ability to pick up the phone and talk to her. But I also felt like I had nothing to say except "I miss you," and "I can't wait to make out again." The conversation was supposed to be full of plans and insight about making great art together. Only Laura could do that. They were going to make a movie together.

Laura and I got into a taxi.

Laura finally broke the silence by saying, "We do have a lot to pack."

I looked at her briefly, thinking, that's not why you didn't want me to have a shot. I stared out the window. It was misting, and the streetlights reflected off the wet sidewalk.

We got out of the car and walked through the bright lobby of the hotel, instantly picking up where we had left off, but in our own voices now.

"I hate it when you drink. You start to say shit you shouldn't. You start to act stupid. You get belligerent and ugly. Just follow my cue. It is my thing, you know. Sometimes you forget that."

"Oh, fuck you. You're on some power trip right now."

"No, I'm just telling you how you get, and you don't want to hear it." She pressed the elevator button twice. She pointed her finger at me. "When you went down to the basement, I said, he's going to want another shot, because I could tell you were getting to that point. And you come up and lo and behold, you ask for another shot. And then the fucked-up thing is that I said to everyone, and they all agreed, that you had had enough. Then they turned around and acted as if we had never had that conversation. 'JT is a grown man.' I mean, really. There you are, dancing around like a fool. Juergen is twice your size, and he can drink. So when you drink with him, trying to keep up, it's like, there you go, off a cliff. And Alice, of all people. Alice just sat there, couldn't look me in the eye."

We entered our room, which had the feeling of a country bed and breakfast, with white walls and blue flowers painted at the corners of the ceiling.

We began to shuffle our piles of clothes around. I threw the clothes Asia had given to me into a heap, along with a polyester tennis skirt, one of the only things I had bought on the trip, at a thrift store in Sweden.

I had made those people choose sides against Laura.

I slammed myself into the bathroom and turned on the tub. I felt righteous, but also a little sorry. I was reminded of a story my mother told me about growing up, about her sister and brother and some of the other kids meeting in the back meadow to strategize about the bully in the neighborhood. She said, we've got to band together against this guy, otherwise he won't leave us alone, and they all agreed. While they were talking he came up behind her and then beat the shit out of her. Her sister and brother stood there with their mouths open and eventually ran away. No one had stood up for her.

This had all gotten too confusing. At the end of every night, I would either hate Laura, or myself. I couldn't stand it anymore. Right then I vowed that I would never be JT again. It was a complication in my life that I didn't need. I would get on the plane, go home, and that would be that.

Laura was finishing up a conversation on the phone. She hung up and gushed how great it had been. Then I heard her slide off the bed and put her face up close to the door. She said, "I am sorry, Savanni. I think we're fighting because our trip together is over." It was true, it was hard to think of the tour ending. But I didn't think this was the reason we were fighting. Laura continued, "I remember when I was young, and my best friend and I would separate, it was easier to end it fighting, it was an easier way to make the break. Listen, I'm sorry."

I sat there and splashed around a bit, trying to stay in my anger. I didn't say I was sorry too, but I rose and unlocked the bathroom door.

TENNESSEE

MASH, THE INTERN, GUIDED ME with impatient steps across the blacktop, clutching his walkie-talkie with his left hand as he spun the volume down. We hugged the sidewalk in front of the diner, bright as a fishbowl, and edged towards the set. I could see our breath misting through the neon lights. I adjusted my black felted fedora tucked under a slim black sweatshirt, and tugged down on the raggedy sleeves of the laquered satin jacket that Asia had given me. It was out of place here. I was cold, and I felt self-conscious in the shiny thin articles of clothing as I edged into the crowd. Everyone wore jean jackets and potato lump sweatshirts and heavy logger's boots. Mash tapped my shoulder, putting his hand up to signal goodbye. He skidded away into the open lot before I had a chance to ask him where Geoff and Laura were. He was such a yankee-in-training, he had no hint of an accent. I actually hadn't heard one yet since I had arrived in Tennessee. I was the only one with a drawl, sort of.

Everyone on the set stood silently. It was the scene in which Jeremiah's mother leaves to go trick, and Kenny, her trucker boyfriend, gets ready to visit other women. The door to a phosphorescent orange cab is open as the cameraman films Kenny, dressed in a bright paisley cowboy shirt with pearl snaps down the front. He wears jeans tight enough that the muscles on his thighs seem to shine and ripple as he rocks to and fro in his seat, spraying his waves of golden hair and aiming down to his package. Such a Laura move. Everyone giggled silently as he adjusted the rear view mirror, combing over the arch of his head, extending his elbow dramatically out and waving the comb through.

I looked around to see if I could catch where Laura and Geoff were standing. They had cameos today. I had flown out a day later than the rest of the family. I was meant to have a cameo tomorrow, which I had binged and starved for accordingly. Months before, when Asia was in pre-production for her film adaptation of *The Heart*, I had asked her if I could work on the costumes. It must have seemed random to her. Though I had given her many pieces that I had made, I couldn't tell her that I was designing clothes. Of course, I had to present the idea via Laura, and she relayed back to me that I could make Asia's outfits only, and I wouldn't be paid for them. I felt a little ashamed at the gall of JT, his sense of entitlement to try for anything, even as a novice. But I was also frustrated that I couldn't have the full opportunity, and that I was only getting this break as JT, and not much of a break at all.

"Just keep all your receipts," Laura had told me.

Suddenly the crowd parted and Asia teetered in wearing a bright blond wig, incandescent red lips, red miniskirt, halter, and stilettos. Something had changed about her. As I looked I realized that it was her eyes—mean and dull like the blunt end of a fire poker.

Someone shouted, "Cut!"

Asia saw me, and her eyes changed. She seemed to droop

slightly in her heels. She grabbed me by the shoulders and leaned with all her weight into me, growling "JT" in an even lower voice then I remembered. She seemed very cold and tired, beyond tired, like she had been tired for weeks. How was this woman directing a film? She could barely speak.

Quietly, I said, "What's going on with you?"

"It's terrible. It's like war. It's very difficult. No one is on my side. They taunt me and undermine me for being a woman, and having an accent."

I noticed that she had a new tattoo on her wrist that said Panos. I examined it carefully like a wound. She said monotonously, "Panos . . . He is amazing with fashion too. He made this. You'll get to meet him." She pointed to a black lump of clothing she had draped over her shoulder like a pet rat. "You will meet him."

I'd rather not, I thought.

"Your ticket . . . Can we change it. Will you stay longer?"

"Um. I don't know," I said flattered. "If I can. Where's Speedie?"

"This is your movie." She responded abruptly.

"Um, yeah, it's mine and yours and um, yeah, a lot of people's," I ventured.

I hadn't noticed, but Brian, Asia and JT's manager, was standing with us, nodding his head as if agreeing with something. His insistence made everything seem meaningless.

"Speedie's at the Kraft truck with Thor." He said.

Asia stared at him for a second and exploded, "Brian!" She had suddenly straightened up, the color returning to her face under cake-y layers of white powder. "I am going to go to the trailer to take off these fucking clothes. Meet me in fifteen minutes. . . . Actually, no. Get Grant over here right now, that piece of shit."

Brian went and got Grant, who came sheepishly with a clipboard. She began to yell at him. "You fucking shithead piece of shit. Are you trying to undermine me? You think you know better? You fucking arrogant piece of shit! You want me to take that money we just lost on that scene out of your paycheck?"

Grant stood with his head bowed. Clearly this wasn't the first time that she had gone ballistic during production.

She turned on her heels, saying in a different voice, "I'm sorry, JT. I'll see you later."

I watched her traipse down the cement. She looked back at me with a nod, flipping her sugar-spun hair. As if he had been waiting for her to leave the whole time, Brian immediately pulled out a cigarette from a pack in his breast pocket.

Grant shrugged, rolling his eyes at Brian.

Brian shrugged back at him. "So you fucked up. Don't worry, man. Life goes on."

Brian led me in between two semis, one with lights decked around it like a porch at Christmas.

"She looks so different." I said to him, thinking she appeared ashen, frenzied, not there.

"I know, right?"

There was a loud hum from a generator. I saw Geoff first. Dressed in dark jeans, an orange-and-brown plaid button-up, and a trucker hat, he stood leaning on one hip like our father always used to stand. Then I saw Thor at his side, his hands wrapped around a Styrofoam cup. Laura was talking to somebody a few feet away, with her hand on her waist. She looked very skinny. She gestured a lot with the other hand. She had gloves on, black with raised puffy skeleton hands and the word "Misfits" scrawled repeatedly across the wrists.

Brian put his hand on Geoff's shoulders.

"Hey, man, you ready, dude? You look awesome."

"Oh, hey! Hey! JT! Thanks. I'm a little nervous. But I look like a bona fide trucker, huh?"

"You look like the real thing, man."

Thor and his mom exclaimed at the same time, "JT!"

Thor hugged me at the waist. He had just had his seventh birthday and seemed to have grown a foot.

Laura and I made eye contact and started to laugh. She hugged me and said, "Babyhead!" holding my neck for a second.

"You should have seen me! I was the waitress, and I had to say, 'More coffee, baby?' and then wink. I got it the first time, but then I had to do it twenty times more. And it got more and more Tourets."

She took a step back, repeating an over-accentuated wink. "More coffee, baby?" She twitched. "But the first time it was very fucking James Bond."

"Mom!"

"I'm sorry, baby. I owe you another dollar."

"You're really racking it up today, Momma," Geoff said.

"Brian is swearing, too."

"I had to give him a twenty just now on reserve! Potter did it, too. You're going to be rich by the end of this trip."

"Potty mouths, all of you." Geoff said.

"I just get f-ing excited." Laura bubbled. "Can you

believe it? Can you believe we're here? Did you go in the diner yet? It's the Dove's Diner. Fucking perfect."

"I've got to see it."

"I had to lip-synch an Italian opera song. I got to stand on top of a table!" Thor said.

"You were so good, Babyhead," Laura said.

"What are you gonna do?" I asked Geoff.

"I gotta pick up a fine lady," he said, grinning.

The thought of Geoff picking up a prostitute tickled me.

"JT," Thor pulled me aside a little bit, "You wearing girls' underwear or boys' underwear right now?"

"Boy's," I said.

He had first asked me this when we were in a hotel corridor getting ice and hot chocolate from the machines. "What if a fan wants your underwear? What if you're wearing girls' underwear?"

"JT's lucky. He can wear either."

Laura turned to me, "You want some hot chocolate? They have all kinds of snacks. Want some trashy candy?" She pulled a Twix and a peanut butter granola bar out of her pocket like she was performing a strip tease.

"I do!" Thor said.

"No, you've had enough today baby," she said firmly.

"Let's go get some hot chocolate for JT."

"When do you go on?" I asked Geoff.

"Pretty soon. We should go back to the hotel cause Thor'll crash pretty soon."

Brian joined us and said, "I can arrange the ride. I'll do it in a little bit. After I go see Asia. You good, JT?"

I nodded. I wanted to go see Asia, too.

Geoff took Thor to hang out with two other kids on the set before his shot, and Laura introduced me to everybody. She said in a low voice, "Can you believe it? Here we are at the truck stop set. I never set foot in a truck stop in my life! It's funny, though, I had this weird déjà-vu sensation as we were walking up, like I had seen it all before, and my past was colliding with my present. I don't know if it was JT talking through me, or what." She paused. Laura often talked to ghosts. Sometimes she spoke to Breece D'J Pancake about why he had committed suicide. Other times she spoke to the singer of an old punk band she used to see as a teenager.

"I never noticed before, but Asia has the same mole on her forehead."

"Same as who?"

"As Sarah. I mean, it's eerie shit. Shit that I didn't tell Asia about, that she has picked up. It's like she's channeling *her*."

"Who?"

"Sarah, JT's mother!"

Brian came back while Laura was standing with me and said, "Asia wants to change your ticket. She wants you to stay. You make her feel grounded."

"Ah, I don't think I can stay through the week." I had to work four shifts at the Thai restaurant to make up for this weekend, plus I had an internship for an independent clothing line called Nisa and had missed it once already to come here. School was impossible with JT's schedule. But I had to work. And I was committed to making clothes.

"She's doing this movie for you," Brian said. I couldn't believe that Asia had said that again. I looked down at the ground.

"Can *you* come back next week?" I asked Laura. She shook her head.

"No. Thor's got a birthday party and a soccer game. But hang on a minute, Brian. Asia's not doing this for JT. That's not true."

"What? She *is* doing it for JT! This is your story, man! She is making your story."

"Brian, don't pull that shit! We all know who she's doing this for. JT has put plenty of time into helping Asia, time that he's not getting paid for." Laura had spent days over the phone working on the script. She had even gone through the revisions. When Laura called Asia and told her that some scenes were just too heavy-handed, she told me that Asia had said, "Now hold on a minute. You're getting kind of Speedie on me. I don't like it when you talk to me like that." Being harsh was associated with Speedie. Didn't JT have the capacity to be harsh or direct?

Brian said, "So what should I tell Asia?"

I was having fun here, and Asia needed me. I would ground her. Me, not JT, I thought. Well, I hoped. But there was the question of missing Valentine's Day with Jonathan. We had been together for close to a year now. He knew all about JT, but not about my feelings for Asia. Or what had happened between us. It wasn't that either of us cared about Valentine's Day, it was more that I felt like I was choosing JT over him, and I felt bad about that. And there was the question of work. The manager at the Thai restaurant had recently asked me, "Do you want to be working here? It doesn't seem like it." Should I risk getting fired? And I was missing my internship. If I came back next week I would miss the sample sale, a venue for local designers. I had already paid for it. Forty dollars—that wasn't a big deal when you thought about it; forty dollars is nothing when you're working. But what if I lost my job?

I felt that familiar pull: should I do that line of blow, start drinking while I'm studying, play hooky, eat something I told myself I shouldn't? I was a fruit fly buzzing around the lip of the honey jar. "Should I come back next week?" I asked Laura.

"The family can't come next week, but I can't tell you what you should do. It's up to you."

"Um, do I have to decide right now?"

"Pretty soon." Brian said. "Because I have to get you the ticket."

"Um . . . Uh. Yeah. All right, next week. I can go for the weekend." Stuck in the amber honey, I had just died again.

The following week, as I flew down to Tennessee, I found out that Mike Pitt would be on the set. He was playing Buddy, one of the only characters sympathetic to Jeremiah in *The Heart*. Out of all of the people I had met as JT, Mike was one with whom I felt the most ease. But I had never been anywhere without Laura backing me up. I was excited. I would be with Asia, Pitt, Potter, who was doing the makeup, and Mel, who was doing the costumes. I felt like JT had real friends. I was to report back to Laura everything that happened.

This time Mash took me to a neighborhood close to Knoxville proper. They were shooting the part of the story in which Jeremiah and his mother are holed up in a speed den with Chester, Sarah's newest boyfriend. They had converted a ramshackle house at the end of a cul-de-sac. Kids from the neighborhood skulked around the trailers, pointing curiously. I spotted Mike. Then I saw one of the kids, a little black boy with tight braided hair, go up to him and gesture at the house. Mike gestured in the same way the boy did. The boy ran off. As I came up he said, "Somehow they got word that the house was going to explode." We hugged, the way I had noticed that men do, the brisk pat on each other's shoulders. I thought of how much I had learned about being a boy since the last time I had seen him. I had learned my "mans" and "dudes," started smoking more to lower my voice, and my mannerisms—and balls—were colder. I always went to the men's bathroom, even in a swarming club with crowds of men. When I walked in with Ben Foster, one of JT's friends, all the men told me that I was in the wrong bathroom. I said easily, "Don't worry. I'm used to this." Ben simply chaperoned me to a stall, saying, "I'll be out here, man." I would say, "Thank you, dude." The emperor's new clothes.

"It's been a long time," Pitt said.

"Yeah, man. Thank you so much for hooking this up for me."

"My pleasure."

Laura had brought at least half of the actors and other celebrities to Asia for the film: Winona Ryder, Peter Fonda, Marilyn Manson, Ben Foster. It was endless work. She was calling up all these Hollywood agents, getting permission for this one or that one, having conference calls with the producers of the film. JT didn't play by Hollywood rules. Laura was doing double time, not sleeping much, negotiating for these actors, and working with Asia to get the script right.

Asia came up to me in a white denim jumper. Her hair was fried blond with black roots growing out, slicked back into a ponytail. Her eyes shone and darted around. She wore dirty white cowboy boots, a pink bandana around her ankle, and no makeup. She hugged me and put her head on my shoulder. "Thank you so much for coming back." I imagined my shoulders to be like Paul Bunyan's, massive and immovable. She pulled away and focused on Pitt. I looked at Mike and suddenly he seemed so childish, like a big baby, when just a few minutes before I had been appreciating his soft mannerisms and limp gestures. Suddenly he became just another entitled brat.

"I like your outfit," I said. She ignored the comment, coyly gesturing with her eyes to Mike. A cloud passed over the sun and I noticed a grey tone to her skin and big bags under her eyes.

Then she came to, registering me after a slight delay.

"Thank you. Panos found and styled it. He left this morning." I think she tried to be casual about him, knowing I was jealous.

"Where is Potter? I need to find Potter." I needed an excuse to escape.

"He's in that trailer." She pointed. "JT, thank you so much for coming back."

I shrugged.

If Laura were here she might have said something like, "I only came for the chocolate. That and a piece of Mike

Pitt's sweet ass." But I couldn't do that. I was too reserved, and it wasn't true. I felt like a paper cut-out with moving appendages, wishing for words to pop out of a bubble above my head.

I edged towards the trailer nestled to the back, hedged in by a fence.

There was Dylan, one of the Sprouse twins. Both were cast as Jeremiah in the film. "Welcome back, JT. Cole is in there getting his hair done by Potter. What do you think? What's it like, watching all this get done?"

I paused. "It's really trippy. It's like, I had this feeling at the truck stop while I was walking up," I drawled a little more, "it was like," I cleared my throat, "I was walking up to my past but it was in my future, or present. Kind of like déjà-vu." I kept my voice low.

"Yeah, it must be strange."

Distracted by Asia and Mike interacting with one another nearby, I didn't say anything.

She looked at me compassionately, as I if to say, "You've been through so much."

"Is that JT? Come in here, you bitch!" Potter sprayed Cole's blond hair, while expertly shielding Cole's face. He bent around to Cole's front and said, "Bitch can be a term of endearment."

Cole sat patiently, his arms straightened out in front of him.

"I'm used to it by now, Potter."

"You're all set. Jiffy Pop!"

"Jiffy Pop!" He put his hands in exclamation points and climbed off the chair.

"I hear Asia wanted you to come back because you ground her. That girl needs some grounding. She was such a monster to me yesterday. I have never been treated like that." He flipped his hair off his forehead.

"Maybe she's getting back at me for frying her hair." He started to get worked up, miming a look of horror, grabbing at his scalp. "I told her to wash her scalp, but she kept it on longer. We used this really intense stuff because we didn't want any trace of brass. I imagine Sarah had perfectly white peroxide hair."

"Mmm."

"But then she didn't take it out soon enough, and her hair turned into poodle's hair. It's grown out, thank God."

"Yeah, I like her new look now."

"I know, she's got the Kurt Cobain look now, in her cute overalls."

"Yeah, she said Panos found them for her," I said in a flat tone.

On my last visit, Geoff, Laura, and I sat at fold-out tables at sunset in the truck stop with Asia and Panos. Panos was lanky, with razored black hair, a pale flat face, and dirty jeans. I think he smoked more cigarettes than he spoke words. I was surprised that Laura hadn't said anything to him about that. The whole set ate dinner together. Well, Asia kind of ate her dinner. She shoved it around her plate, then went for dessert. Her hair was fuzzy blond, like a teddy bear. She looked ashen and had scratches all over her neck. She wore a million different colors of ratted black. "It is like war here. Everyone is against me," she kept repeating. I didn't know what to say.

"What use is it, thinking it's like war?" Laura asked her. I was grateful she was there because I didn't know how to handle Asia's apocalyptic moods.

"It's not strategic, I know. But I cannot have all these assholes challenging me every time we try to do something. It is like they are constantly trying to trip me, because I am a woman directing. And I am Italian. I don't forget shit like this." It was like she was playing battleship in her head, like she was in her own fantasy world. Her jaw protruded for a second as if she was locking it and grinding her teeth. She frothed the whipped cream with her plastic spoon, and wolfed down canned peaches. She began to rattle off a list of everyone who was against her, who was a "piece of shit." They were all in earshot. I saw their backs tense up.

"Yeah, I guess, Mel and she have worked it out," Potter said forlornly. "I just hope I'm not next, 'cause I won't stand for that shit. I will walk off." He made his eyes big at me as if I were going to tell him not to.

"I am sorry, JT. I will walk off."

Potter reached for his pack of cigarettes and motioned for me to come outside with him.

"Anyway, Marilyn Manson is coming."

"When?"

"Next week." I would miss him. He was going to play one of Sarah's baby daddies, a Jesus freak who molests Jeremiah. Poor JT. I think Marilyn had sent Laura one of his paintings. At the other trailer, Mel was spray painting leather jackets with stencils for Chester's band; it looked like eagle wings and skeletons. Laura had hooked me up with Mel for a Knoxville thrift shopping date. There would also be a visit from the local chocolatier tomorrow. Fortunately, I was beginning to like chocolate.

They shot all day and on into the night, doing thousands of takes. The cameraman seemed very methodical. You could see why people working on movies were either heavy smokers or fat. I had to admit, Pitt was a good actor. I noticed throughout the day he had picked up my mannerisms and certain intonation. It made me cringe the way he said certain words like "soon," the same way I said it. I thought I sounded autistic. He wasn't making fun of me either. He was earnest, the little fucker. He stayed close to me throughout most of the evening.

Asia came up to us as it got later.

"So you both will stay in my apartment. I have a couch that pulls out into a bed." Well, who was supposed to sleep on that? What was she thinking? A threesome? No, I thought to myself, I don't want him there. Why can't he stay in a hotel? He won't ground her. He'll distract her. I could feel the blood rushing to my face. Was it time for a JT tantrum?

When we got back to Asia's apartment she changed into cotton navy pajamas with white anchors embroidered on them and a white v-neck T-shirt. She combed her hair and wiped the powder from her face. I sat on the couch reading Laura's signed copy of Lewis Nordan's *Music of the Swamp*. I couldn't put it down, and it gave me something to do and talk about.

"It's really good, Asia. I'll give it to you when I'm done." Give away Laura's signed copy?

"I would like that."

Smoking cigarettes, Pitt sat against the couch. He didn't need to have anything to do. I could feel us both leaving our books and cigarettes behind to watch her wipe the powder off her face. When she was done Mike picked up his guitar. He held his gaze on her. What a ham. I knew Asia had a thing for musicians, and I wanted to stop him before it began.

Intercept, quickly, I thought. I focused in on his gold chain. "Where'd you get that?"

He stopped playing. "Hugo Boss. I modeled for them and they gave me all this free shit."

"Huh." As he began to strum again I said, "I gave my love a chicken that had no bone."

"What?"

"Was it fun?" What a stupid question, and it wasn't working as a distraction. "So when are you going to have an album out?"

He ignored me and began to reel off different ballads. I needed voodoo to get him to stop playing. To get him to realize he should get his own room. This was a lost cause.

I decided to take a shower. I sat down in the tub and looked down. I'm a fucking Sasquatch. I bet they both just naturally have no excess body hair. No cellulite. No scars.

I started to shave myself maniacally. The hair got stuck in the razor and I had to keep pulling it out to keep it from getting clogged. It clogged anyway. I had ruined Asia's razor. I could already feel the sting of razor burn, trickles of blood glistening on my shins.

When I opened the door, Asia and Mike were on her bed locked in an embrace. They parted slightly.

"Well, goodnight," I mumbled.

They said, "Goodnight" in unison, too fast.

I curled up on the couch and fumed. He wouldn't even be here without me. Well, without JT. I tried to read a little more, but I couldn't focus. It was horrible to hear them, to hear Asia's scratched vocal chords. I wondered if Pitt was a bottom. Asia was kind of a toppy-bottom. Would they ever calm down? I curled back up into my ball. What a mind-fuck for poor JT.

The next morning, I struggled to keep my eyes closed while Asia brushed her teeth and giggled in the bathroom with Mike. She emerged and slammed the door behind her. As I opened my eyes and squinted them back shut, I saw her throw her bag over her shoulders like she was walking down a New York street, her pointy black shoes leaving imprints in the rug.

I opened my eyes and lay there, listening to the hum of the air conditioner. I heard Mike get up and pee, clear his throat, and spit. He came out stretching his arms, and said, "Asia told us to call when we want to be picked up. I've got to be on set at ten-thirty." I lay there, the blankets binding me like a straight jacket. Fucking asshole.

"What time is it now?"

"Almost eight," he said, sounding like he had a mouth full of bread.

"I think we could sleep a little longer."

"Okay."

"I'll wake you up again in forty minutes."

"Okay." I said blankly.

When we arrived on the set Asia pushed a little wooden box into my hand and said, "Will you give this to Mike?"

"Sure."

Great, so I was there not only to ground her, but to pass love letters and drugs to her new lover. As she left I opened the box and saw a little piece of paper with a lipstick mark and the same heart with an arrow and flames that she had once written on a love letter to JT. I didn't need to read it. I knew what it said.

After lunch she asked me into her trailer.

"JT, what do you think about this line: 'Somebody fucked their nigger and you got the nose to prove it.' Do you think we should take that out and put something else? What would be appropriate? It seems beside the point, you know? We could say 'someone fucked their slave'? What do you think, would that be a better way to say it?"

"Um, you could say somebody fucked their neighbor, or you could just leave it out." I didn't know what to say. I was obsessing about last night. I couldn't be bothered with script details.

She stayed in her bathroom a long while.

When she came out, her forehead was glistening. What drugs was she doing? I wondered.

"Yeah, maybe we will just leave it out. I try, JT. I try to hold onto as much of your text as possible. Sometimes, over the phone, I don't recognize you. You sound like someone else. But that someone is still full of amazing guidance."

Desperate to change the subject, I offered, "Do you want to read this Lewis Nordan book later? I'm done with it."

"Sure, I'll read it."

"I think you'll like it a lot. There is tons of stuff about the South in there."

"Okay . . . I've got to get back to the set, JT."

"I know."

After she left, I began to cry. I felt sorry for myself, and strangely, for JT as well. And the nightmare wasn't over yet.

TINC

THE AIRPORT SHUTTLE DROPPED ME OFF a few doors down from the Natoma Street loft. As I hoisted my duffel bag on my shoulder, I heard the zipper tear. The bag gaped and buckled at the spine. I sighed dramatically. Everything was literally falling apart.

I fumbled for my keys at the side of my bag. Climbing the stairs, I dumped my bag on the ground in the back room where Jonathan and I slept. I headed straight for the toilet, then I heard Jonathan's shuffle.

From the main room he called out, "You back?"

"Yeah."

I waited in the entrance to meet him. As he came up to me, I was angry with myself for going off to Tennessee to be with a fucking lunatic.

"I missed ya! How was it?"

"I don't know . . . I guess it was kind of fucked up. Asia is . . . having problems that I can't help with."

"It's hard to see a friend go through something like that."

"Yeah. I mean, I don't think I can do it anymore."

"Try to help Asia? Or be JT?"

"Be JT. I mean, it's all too weird and exhausting. The lines are too blurred. I don't know how to explain it. I feel like it's taking over my life. And I'm sorry I missed Valentine's Day . . ."

"Don't worry about it. I'll take you out for sushi tonight." He grinned, leaning on the door and crossing one leg over another. He wore his tweed paper-boy hat and new glasses.

I said, quickly "No, my treat."

"So, it's decided? You're not going to do it anymore?"

"It's over."

His eyes softened. "Proud of you, man. I wasn't going to say anything but I'm glad you've come to that conclusion on your own."

"Yeah. It took a while."

"It did. And I couldn't tell you what to do. You knew how I felt about it. But we have to reach decisions on our own."

Jonathan had always disapproved of my being JT. For most straight men it would have been the threat of his girlfriend pretending she was a boy, but that wasn't the part that bothered him. He just couldn't see why I was doing it. I wasn't being paid very well. He could see that I was conflicted about it. After each time he talked to Laura on the phone, he would say to me, "She's getting over on you." He couldn't understand why I would dye my eyebrows for her, or more importantly, why I would give myself over to her idea. He thought the whole thing brought out my neurosis. Either I really wanted to do it and couldn't just say so. Or I didn't want to do it, but couldn't stand up for myself. Either way, it bothered him, and in the beginning especially, he considered breaking up with me over it.

But a few months after being together, he came with Geoff, Laura, and me to a New York reading. Laura had stayed up for weeks arranging the event, talking on the phone excitedly with everyone involved. The reading was set in a club where girls in mermaid costumes swam around in a huge fish tank with oxygen tubes taped up their backs. Laura had as always personally invited slews of different artists to read for JT. At various times there had been Lou Reed, Tatum O'Neal, Winona Ryder, Marianne Faithful, Harper Simon, Rosario Dawson, Courtney Love, Sharon Olds, and Mary Karr. At this point in JT's career, he didn't read aloud at his own events in the States yet. He would stand in the back of the room, twitching, while others read his work for him.

That night, Jonathan seemed a little freaked out by my change in identity, my awkward body language and low-voiced thank-yous. But I think he was amazed that hundreds of people came to meet and connect with JT. I got the feeling that he finally understood why it was so hard for me to stop being JT, even when it had spiraled out of control. In the hotel corridor, I watched him sit cross-legged in the hall with Courtney Love, who was sheathed in a sheer pastel dress that hung carelessly from one shoulder. Like a dysfunctional fairy, she examined his palm, telling him many good things about his future. He grinned from ear to ear. As we walked back to our hotel room he looked at me and said, "It's like walking into Narnia."

The next day I called each person in my family and told them, "I quit." Every one of them had the same reaction: "Good. Get on with your life." I called Laura last. I told her about all the different people I had met on the set of

The Heart. I told her about Asia consulting me on the script change. And then I told her about the night in the apartment with Mike Pitt.

"It's not that I mind that they like each other," I said, though I did. "It was just rude. Why make me stay with them? Why didn't she set me up in a different hotel room if she wanted to do that? I didn't need to be put through that. And what if I really were JT? What a mind fuck! She's sick!" Part of me thought, look who's talking.

Laura listened, making sympathetic noises and mewing, "I'm so sorry that happened to you." We talked a little while longer, and I kept trying to find a way to tell her that I was going to quit. But I didn't. We hung up, and I stared at the phone for a few seconds. Then I picked it up again and called her back. "I think I need to quit."

"I understand," she said, as if she had known I was going to say it. I didn't tell her about the Lewis Nordan book yet.

I had seventeen hundred dollars in my savings account from my JT outings, and I was working four times a week at the restaurant.

One evening at work, a bunch of us were standing around chatting and joking with our boss. Without thinking, I asked him if he wanted to finance my clothing project.

"Show me what you have," he said, calling my bluff.

The next day I dropped off a package of one-of-a-kind pieces in cotton voile, printed with a black-and-white cheetah pattern, along with some drawings I had made at City College in my patterning class. He gave the package to his wife, Pauline.

The following day, my boss handed me an envelope with a note on quarter-inch graph paper, in the sleekest hand-writing I had ever seen. "Dearest Savannah . . ." Pauline wrote that she could see where these ideas were going, and she was very interested in becoming my financial partner. I gasped when I read the words, "Please call me after work."

I had always liked Pauline, but I had never met her out-side of the restaurant. She was a Thai woman about a foot or so shorter than me. That day we met she wore high-waisted men's trousers with platform shoes, and a baggy cobalt undershirt made out of silk. Her deep brown hair was twisted up into a half pompadour. I liked the way she had dusted silver eye makeup all the way around her eyes. She smelled like lavender.

We sat down at my kitchen table and went over what we would need to begin a clothing business. I was excited about embarking on this project—it had nothing to do with JT. At the same time, I was aware of my influences. Much of my passion had been spurred by the opportunity to wear designer clothing as JT. One huge inspiration had been Gary Graham. After fawning over his clothes repeat-edly, Mike Potter gave me Gary's phone number while I was in New York. I called him using my JT accent, a rarity back then—Laura usually made all the calls. Gary invited me over. Laura stayed behind at the hotel. I walked down to Tribeca to meet Gary in his studio, and found him hunched over the counter, brow furrowed, examining a leather jacket inside out. His lips were pursed. He wore a paisley shirt rolled up at the sleeves, and his hair looked as if he had been pulling it in different directions.

"What're you workin' on?" I asked.

"This coat . . . I think I've made it harder than it is," he said wistfully. "I've been at it for days now, and we're going into production with it soon."

"Is that the sample?"

"The fourth sample."

"Seems like hard work."

"It is, but it's rewarding," he said earnestly. He got off his stool and folded up the jacket. I felt very comfortable around Gary, and stopped worrying about my accent and my behavior. He walked me through the racks.

"Judging by your clothes, I would think you know what you like, so pick out some stuff. But I also have a suit. . . . Do you wear seersucker?"

"I love seersucker!"

"It's kind of weird, so I didn't put it on the floor, but I think it would look great on you," he said, gesturing wildly as he walked behind a white muslin curtain. He came out with a classic blue-and-white seersucker, but it wasn't at all conventional. The coat had a princess seam with layered tails, and came with a pair of baggy pants to match. I squealed.

"Oh good, you like it! Try it on. Did you pick out some other stuff?"

"No, not yet." This clothing was expensive, which made me nervous.

"Well you're going to need a shirt to go underneath the suit . . . something like this?"

He went around to the racks, pulling one of almost every piece.

As I tried the clothes on, Gary stayed outside the dressing room, explaining details of dye and construction. He confided the ways he would have changed each piece. His way of working was completely hands-on. He had a dye lab in the basement, made his own labels, and signed each piece.

I picked out a suit, a shirt, a jacket, pants, and a quilted short vest that felt like feudal armor. Then Gary led me around, showing me how everything was made. I decided right then that he was my idol. I wanted to be a designer just like him.

This was all part of my education. Interning with Nisa had given me a pragmatic sense of the process of clothing design. I knew Pauline and I needed to make a sample line out of fabrics we could buy repeatedly. We needed a catalogue, and we needed patterns. Eventually we would have to do a trade show. Pauline and I set up our fictitious business name under "Tinc." In Thai, tinc means to throw away. We opened a bank account and Pauline deposited 2,000 dollars. This money would be used to make the fall line and to pay overhead for the office; any extras came out of my pocket.

My friend Brenda had rented an office space in the Grant building on the corner of Seventh and Market, to work on her own line. The rent was $250 a month, and I offered to split it with her. We shared the first suite on the landing of the second flight of wrought-iron stairs. Oasis, a healthcare clinic for the mentally ill, was stationed directly across from us, and the Bike Coalition was down the hall. Black stenciled letters adorned the frosted glass doors of each suite. The building looked like a set in *The Maltese Falcon*.

We hired a friend to help us build a sixty-inch cutting and patterning table with a shelf on the bottom to store bolts of fabric. As we built the tables, people wandered in to see what we were doing. A lawyer barged in and asked, "How much to fix my canvas yacht covers?"

"We don't do that kind of thing," I said indignantly. "We're not menders."

Once completed, the table took up half of the room. There was just enough space to slide in and make our patterns on either side of the table. Outside our window we also had a balcony of sorts, the roof of a donut shop. We used this setting for our photo shoots and as our dye lab, which consisted of a hose, a tumbler of salt, and a few buckets of paint.

Once the studio was set up, Brenda and I drove down to Los Angeles to hunt for fabric at a textile show. We quickly found out that most of the fabrics at the show were sold at a thousand-yard minimum. We heard that there were jobbers making smaller sales nearby. We found one called "B and J" down an alley, in a warehouse jammed to the ceiling with bolts of fabric. It was oppressively hot and dusty. The man at the front had hair on his arms so thick that one could have parted and combed it. He handed each of us a pair of scissors to cut swatches of the fabrics we wanted.

"I do not sell by the yard, only by the bolt, ladies." I watched the man's eyes crawl up the slits of Brenda's orange running shorts as she disappeared into the depths of the warehouse. I turned around to avoid making eye contact with him.

None of these fabrics seemed right. I was reminded of the time Laura and I had met with Ennio Capasa of Costume National. I had been struck by the fabrics. The pieces were displayed on vaulted lacquered pipes, and were made of rubberized cottons, destroyed silks, and veils of cashmere. Ennio picked up a heavy winter jacket and explained that he'd hired a factory to blend a special weave of wool with metal to emblazon the back of his coats with gold-and-copper peacocks. Unlike Gary Graham's work, Ennio's pieces weren't examples of hands-on artistry; they were sleek and seamless. I had a feeling it would take me awhile to get to that point, if ever.

Towards the end of the corridor in B and J, I found a pair of cream-and-black bolts of canvas and a peacock-colored silk taffeta. Close enough. Down another corridor I found some cotton lycras, a micro-modal material, and a bolt of nude rip-stop.

When I returned, the man was drinking mint tea, his legs propped up on a bolt of fabric. Maps of sweat bled through his collared pink shirt at his chest and armpits. He disapprovingly took one of my swatches and pointed to a sign that read, "Do not swatch the silk."

"I didn't know it was silk."

"What are you doing here then?"

"I am here to buy fabric."

"Only by the bolt, not by the yard. This is for real clothing-makers. Not hobbyists."

Why is it that no one takes young women seriously? JT

didn't go around encountering this bullshit. JT didn't even have to say anything. But I had to state my mission to every person I met, reassuring them that I was indeed serious, that I was not wasting their time.

"Do you want my business or not?" I held the swatch in my hand, rubbing the silk and praying that he wouldn't say no.

"Sweetie, I just want to make sure you know what this place is. Is this all you want?"

"Yes."

He called out, "Mauricio! Mauricio!"

The owner handed him the swatches, and he went adeptly into the forest, returning with each bolt. They weighed at least forty pounds each. Mauricio was dripping sweat by the time he had picked them all out. I was scared of the inconvenience of these bolts, how much space they took up, and the amount of underpaid labor that had gone into making and transporting them. What was I getting myself into? Mauricio helped us pack the fabric into our rental car, the bolts falling over each other like pick-up-sticks. We gave him a tip and drove off.

Biting our fingernails, we watched the sun set. This is the beginning, I felt. Every oldie on the radio spoke to me. Everything was a sign. In the back of my mind I was thinking, I finally have found something in my life besides being JT.

I stayed up every night for weeks making patterns for the fall season. I hired a sample-maker, a woman named Dianna from Vietnam. I ripped apart my favorite sailor shirt and Italian warm-up jacket. I made two shirts, a pair of canvas jodhpurs, and a rain slicker inspired by something that Asia had given me. I hired a patternmaker to make a jumpsuit out of cream canvas.

Once a week I went to a San Francisco boutique that had pioneered some local designers. I hoped they might try out Tinc. When I finally got an appointment with the owner, I said that I would bring in our catalogue—only I didn't have one. I begged my friend Naomi to be my model, and my mother to be my photographer. We pulled it off in two days. Pauline came in with me for the appointment wearing a stylish black windbreaker. I was so proud to have her with me. We wrote our first order.

Going door-to-door seemed like the best way to get the next orders. Brenda and I planned a trip to New York to try to sell our clothes to boutiques there. We had made lists of buyers, hoping to set up appointments in advance. But every call ended with the words, "not interested." Click.

I wished I could be more like JT, that I could charm people despite my shyness. If I could only contact the people JT had met: Calvin Klein, Bianca Jagger, Juergen Teller, Courtney Love. If only I could ask Winona Ryder to wear my clothes. But I couldn't ask. I didn't want to ask. This was my life, and that was his.

Without any appointments, we flew to New York, deciding to try the pitch in person. We stayed with my former roommate Shane in a little flat on Henry Street in a sixth-floor walk-up.

In the brute February wind we walked through Manhattan neighborhoods with our color copied catalogues.

Our bags were stuffed with samples just in case a buyer challenged us and said, "Okay, let's see it." It was a whole new way of traveling. I found it vaguely masochistic and very exciting, though in the end our trip did not bring the results I had hoped for. My savings had dwindled into nothing. The money from Pauline was two-thirds gone. We hadn't even done production yet for our one order. With just one six hundred dollar order, there was no way to break even. I placed some pieces in consignment shops, but consignment moves too slowly. I needed twice the amount of money that Pauline had given to Tinc originally to do a trade show. I needed four thousand dollars.

The phone rang twice in a row.

I pulled myself out of bed, and ran to the kitchen.

"Hello?"

"Oh good, you're there." It was my sister, Hennessey. "I wasn't sure if I should call you. That's why I called and hung up. Sorry. Anyway, Laura called me several times. The film producers of *The Heart* really want JT to go to Cannes for the premiere. Laura thinks she has the money lined up to make it worth your while, but she said she couldn't ask you directly."

"How much do you think is 'worth it'?"

"I don't know. I mean, I guess it's relative. Probably more than you've ever made."

"What do you think I should do?"

"Well, to be honest, I didn't even want to tell you about it. But I felt like that wasn't right either. It's your decision to make."

"Maybe if it's enough, I'll do it just one more time."

Just once more. I sounded like an alcoholic taking just one more drink.

I vacillated for a while, then called Laura.

"I knew I shouldn't ask you, but you could make four thousand dollars in four days," Laura said solemnly.

My stomach clenched. Four thousand dollars.

"There is one condition though. I told people that JT couldn't go out to parties because he was afraid of having a relapse. So, you're not allowed to drink. It will make the producers nervous, and they're the ones paying JT to do this press. And between you and me, you don't do as well when you drink."

Here we go, not even a minute into being JT again and Laura was telling me that I had problems, and what to do about them. I was annoyed, but I knew she was right. When I drank I said things that JT shouldn't.

"Asia is on the wagon, too. So you won't be the only one."

Asia. I felt the icicle beginning to drip.

"Okay, I'll go."

CANNES

RIDING SHOTGUN IN THE BIG WHITE VAN, Brian Young surfed his Blackberry while Laura and I sat sandwiched between Geoff and Thor in the back. The tawny plains shimmered in the heat; occasionally a blackbird flew up in front of us. We had arrived at a hotel situated in the arid mountains northwest of Cannes the afternoon before. As we got out of the car with our luggage, the producers hefted cardboard boxes of what looked to be about four pounds of apples, three loaves of wheat bread, four cartons of soy milk, one jar of almond butter, one jar of jam, and twelve bars of chocolate. They had offered to get us some snacks for our room, not realizing what that would entail.

Lilly Bright, one of the producers, and her boyfriend, Brad, carried the boxes. I could feel them fuming. They had scoured the health food stores in Cannes to find all of JT's requests.

"We couldn't get you the organic almonds," Lilly said cuttingly.

Speedie jokingly said, "No organic almonds! Take it back!"

Lilly scowled. Laura quickly said, "Thank you, this stuff makes a big difference. We really appreciate all your effort, Lilly."

Lilly looked like she was going to drop the box.

"You want me to take that?" I asked. Best to act like I wanted this stuff, right?

"No. I'm just going to put it down here," she flashed me a polite smile.

Asia sauntered up. She stood barefoot in the doorframe. "What's with all this stuff?"

I shrugged as though I had no part in it. I reminded myself that I was going to keep my distance from her. My head jerked back. I'm not falling for her again—her bony, bare feet, her sloppy hair, her winded speech—I told myself. Once I got home from Tennessee, I wouldn't let myself fantasize about her anymore. I knew that chapter was over.

We set the boxes down in a fairy tale cottage, which had a wood-shingled round roof and a window seat overlooking a trellis of grape vines. It was a suite. The bedroom had a porch overlooking a gulch now in shadow. On the closet door hung three garment bags marked with the Costume National insignias. Laura and I rushed past the boxes and luggage, unzipping the garment bags feverishly. The designer had flown out specifically for the premiere of *The Heart* to dress JT. He had sent a freight of clothes for all of us to wear. For Laura, a lambskin trench, lace undershirts, a Wonder Woman belt, long skirts with hoops, and kid gloves. Geoff got a sheer pink dress shirt and sharkskin pants. I picked out a thin wool sharply lapelled jacket, matching pants, an onyx vest woven with metal, and a black shirt with sequins sewn down the front. This was how clothes should feel: my posture instantly changed, I enunciated, I didn't worry about my body. I could joust. If I took off my jacket I could wrestle. I was ready for anything. It was like finding a new part of myself that had been lost at birth, my full potential reclaimed.

I was helping Laura snap on a pair of racing gloves when Roberta, one of the producers, came in. Everything was spread all around the room. She began to pluck pieces off the couch and love seat. "You guys have done well for yourselves! Look at this stuff! It is fa-bu-lous! JT, you look fantastic! Oh, you all look fantastic!" She found another pair of gloves on the windowsill.

"Can I have these?" Her eyes darted around.

"No!" Laura countered. "We don't even know what we get to keep yet."

"Please?"

"No, Roberta!" Laura said grabbing the gloves.

"What are you wearing, Asia?" Roberta asked, her tone still a little hurt. Asia had slipped into the room quietly.

"Fendi, you know. I still have that contract with them," she said with an exasperated tone, then turned and left. I turned my head away from her direction so my eyes couldn't follow her.

Roberta left as well.

Laura watched them go and then laughed under her breath, "What a hustler!"

As the vans descended over the lazy hills, the driver put on a Beatles CD. Laura and Thor sang along, "I am the Walrus. Goo goo g'joob." The garment bags of finery hung like drapes, swinging back and forth with each curve. Asia and I were to walk the red carpet before the screening of *The Heart*. As the van crested a hill we saw the ocean and an enclave of high rises crowding up against a crop of beige sand. We reached the lowlands, and suddenly traffic came to a stop. Brian cursed. Apparently *Fahrenheit 9-11* had just screened, and a group of Iraq War protesters clotted the streets, drumming and chanting. We crawled behind them. Peppering the crowd of tie-dye and banners and peace signs were little green ears. "*Shrek II* fans!" Thor pointed out.

"Can't you just run them over?" Brian growled, "You guys are going to miss everything. We have seventeen minutes to get you there. Fuck!"

Suddenly his phone rang, and he replied, "Right. Okay, that's what we'll do, man. Okay, he's going to come right out. I'll bring his clothes now."

Brian said, "Okay, JT. We can get you there faster if we get you out of the car here, walk you to the hotel room to change, do your makeup, and then deliver you by foot to the red carpet."

"And where do we meet you?" Laura asked vehemently.

"I'll call you. You'll probably only be a block away by the time we're done."

"Brian, we are not missing the premiere, do you understand?"

"No, you won't."

"There's no fucking way, Brian," Laura insisted.

Geoff pulled my clothes off the hook and passed them to Brian, who swung the van door open with such force that it bounced back and hit Geoff in the elbow. Industry fervor. The clothes sparkled in their plastic bag. Brian started to herd me down the street to the hotel. It was hot out and smelled like gasoline and ocean. You could feel the brightness of the sea reflecting the sun. Brian was body-blocking now, pushing people aside, using a lot of force for such a little person. I could see Asia and *The Heart*'s press manager running up ahead of us. We passed boys in polo shirts and girls in dresses, all wearing ogre ears. We made our way across a road divider shaded by an even row of palm trees, their red fruit littering the well-kept grass. The *Shrek* fans moaned with excitement. Up ahead, on top of the premiere theater, a football goal-sized screen had been erected. The green ogre princess shimmered, and then Cameron Diaz appeared in a white evening gown, waving to fans on the red carpet.

Brian hurriedly dragged me into the hotel lobby, which was like a dim capsule, air-conditioned and sound-proofed. Asia's manager pressed the elevator button. We all watched as the digitized numbers stood still and then flipped down through the floor numbers. Brian's foot tapped impatiently. A group of people, talking loudly, exited the elevator, reeking of perfume. We reached our reserved room, where a brawny man with an orange spray-tan stood at attention with his palette and brushes laid out on a mahogany coffee table. Asia wiggled into her dress, leaving the zipper open. She sat down for makeup. The manager pulled my clothes out of the garment bag.

"I'll meet you downstairs," Brian called out, rushing off somewhere.

The manager didn't reply. He exclaimed to Asia, "I love this! Asia! Fantastic!"

"It's such a boring dress!" Asia moped.

"It is not! It is classic. It says everything you want it to say!" he clapped his hands together. It was a '40s-inspired cocktail dress in black silk crepe.

"Who made this?" he asked.

"Fendi," she said, chagrined.

"Oh-la-la," the makeup artist murmured.

"I feel like it's so conventional and . . . prissy. I am doing it because of my contract with Fendi. It is to feed my child."

"I love it! Darling! No excuses. Love it. Now, JT, you don't have a cummerbund, do you?"

I shook my head. My shirt had sequins embroidered on it—wasn't that enough?

He clucked his tongue.

"You will not look right without a cummerbund. Do you want mine?"

He pulled a bright red satin one from his Vuitton saddlebag.

"No. I . . . Let me just put my clothes on."

I went into the bathroom.

When I came out he said, "Can't you take that silly wig off?"

"No, I can't do that."

"And those silly sunglasses?"

"He won't." Asia said through pouty lips as the makeup artist applied the finishing touches. Her face was powdered like a truffle.

"Oddball. But you're right, you don't need that cummerbund. Oh *merde*, we have to go. Are we ready?"

Asia looked in the mirror.

"You put too much makeup on me! It makes me look like a transvestite!"

He had done her eyebrows a little heavily.

"I just wanted you to look glamorous! You must look good for the cameras," the makeup artist said defensively.

Asia stood up, windshield wiping her face with her hands. As she examined herself in the mirror, she cried, "I'm fat!"

"You *are* not," I said in a low voice.

"Darling, you are not fat! Though we all want to slim down for the cameras." The manager lifted his hands and glided them down his hips. "Puts ten pounds on, Darling!" he said, zipping up the back of her dress. She rolled her eyes at him as if he were her great aunt and she were a teenager.

At one point the night before, when we met outside on the stone steps of the villa, Asia had grabbed at her belly through her layers of T-shirt and moaned, "I am so fat," in the same tone. She wore sneakers and her Bic-scrawled jeans and a dowdy sweater. Her hair fell in her eyes. She plunged into her pasta carbonara, saying with a full mouth, "God, I need a glass of wine to go with this." I agreed with her, and she gave me a look like, "You don't need it like I need it." I had ordered the crudités, an anorexic meal consisting of whole radishes, endive, carrots, and different kinds of anchovy paste. I could feel her staring at my raw vegetables, and suddenly she said, "You, with your Capoeira, and your healthy meals." She had never mentioned my Capoeira or vegetables before. I was surprised she had noticed. I was still the same size, which in my mind was never skinny enough for her to be attracted to me.

For a moment I felt kind of smug, though. There she was: toppled, humbled. I thought, ungenerously, "Welcome to *our* club." Then I caught myself shift to motherly worry, thinking, "Better that you are eating than doing drugs."

I had recently gone again to an Overeaters Anonymous meeting. But again, I had not been ready to utter that preliminary sentence, "My name is Savannah and I am a compulsive overeater." Was I really compulsive? And why couldn't I talk about it? I still hadn't told my mother or sister about any of it yet. When I went to the meeting, and the members exploded back in my face, "Hi Savannah!" I felt like saying, "Don't call me that." I wished I had given them a false name.

I had hoped I could fix this problem myself. But my attempts weren't really solutions. I thought, for instance, that I should just become obsessed with something else. But I exercised too much to get heavily into drugs or alcohol. Since I love to poke myself with needles while I listen to a really great song, I thought maybe I should consider cutting. Sitting with Asia, I wondered if she had always had issues with her body. And it made me wonder, is it always going to be like this? Can't we live without some obsession, or compulsion, or addiction breathing down our necks? I looked up to Asia and Laura, two exceedingly powerful women, both acclaimed for their art. Well, Laura's case was different, but you see what I'm getting at. Didn't we figure it out at a certain point?

Asia, the manager, and I piled back into the elevator. Asia wiggled her hips, shaking her underwear down underneath her tight dress. We met Brian in the lobby, hunched over his phone, and ventured back into the crowd. We crossed the street and forced our way into the nucleus of ogre ears.

The manager stood behind us murmuring, "Now, walk with confidence. You look stunning, Asia. Make sure you pay respect to the Madame and Monsieur at the top of the stairs."

I could see flashing lights as the gates opened. The manager gave me a little push. In front of us was a tiered structure, stacked with a tidal wave of paparazzi. The lights were blinding. All I could see were white blotches, as if my eyeballs had been melted by exploding light. I began to walk very fast. Asia grabbed my hand and slowed me down. Her touch induced something strange in me. A calm settled into my fingertips and up into my torso. She walked very gradually, stopping every few steps. She dropped my hand and put hers on her waist, posing and smiling.

I followed her, hamming up JT's nervousness. I was little JT, someone who didn't belong, walking with a short gait like Charlie Chaplin, turning his head from side to side as if he were looking for someone. I even looked up at the sky, thinking, ham it up if you want to. No one can tell who you are or how you got here. Between the dark glasses, the gaucho hat, the wig, and the slumped shoulders, JT was impenetrable. We made our way past the wall of cameras up the steps to a regal man and woman. Were these the founders of the Cannes Film Festival? Royalty? Asia gracefully said her thank-yous. I mumbled my own, "Thanks," to the exalted ones. The woman strained to hear what I was saying and I snapped my head back as if a dog were trying to bite at me. She pulled back too, pursing her lips, a little confused. We made our way out, towards the back of the building.

"You were fantastic, Asia. Ciao!" screamed Asia's manager.

All of a sudden Laura, Geoff, and Thor appeared.

"Baby, you were fantastic! There you were, walking in front of Angelina Jolie!"

"You looked nervous," Thor piped in.

Brian came up behind us and tugged on my sleeve, "We need to get to the premiere. Come on."

"Thor and I aren't going to stay for the movie. We have an ice-cream date. We'll see you soon. Break a leg, JT." Geoff said. I gave them each a kiss.

"Come on, we've got to go," Brian exclaimed impatiently, pulling on my hand. Laura followed as he dragged me through a marble lobby, up some stairs, around a corner, and up some more stairs. He held his Blackberry out like a compass.

"We need to split up," he said to Laura, "and get JT and Asia in first."

Now the manager led us, while Brian blocked Laura. I couldn't understand why everything was so complicated. I could hear Laura bickering with Brian. We entered the dark theater. People with flashlights directed us to the front of the audience. A spotlight descended onto us as we walked up the stairs in front of the screen. I kept my head down and began the old shiver.

Asia recited a succinct list, thanking everyone who'd made the movie happen. She passed the microphone over to me. The shadow of my hat swallowed it up in darkness. I could vaguely see silhouettes of people, their eyes flashing like cats in the dark.

"..."

"... I want cha all to watch this with open hearts." A little voice. Timorous, twangy, girlie.

"It's a ... very ... courageous movie. ... *Vive la resistance!*" I had decided to say that when I was on the airplane over.

People began to clap, and I followed Asia down off the stage.

Just then, I recognized a silhouette moving down the aisles in wrestling boots, sunglasses, and a cloche hat. I knew that walk. I had followed it when we entered the Virgin VIP lounge in our pajamas, the Ritz-Carlton breakfast buffet—so many places I never expected to be. Brian trailed behind her. Asia and I joined her and we all slid into our reserved seats. Laura grabbed my hand and whispered hoarsely, "I almost wasn't let in because of shit-bird over here. Had to tell him a few things, but we made it! I love you!"

"I love you, too."

She reached over me and grabbed Asia's hand and said, "I love you!" to her in the same tone. Asia gave her a cock-eyed look and then squeezed it back. As the lights dimmed, I territorially kept my arm on the divider, my hand next to Asia's. Maybe we would hold hands. I felt the old fantasies stewing. Maybe we would fuck, maybe we would fall in love, maybe we would elope. A dream from the night before flashed before my eyes. Asia and I were standing together on a cliff overlooking the sea. The afternoon light flashed gold on the water. Cicadas ground their wings so loud that we could barely hear one another, but it didn't matter. The theater's digital surround sound boomed, and Jeremiah came up on the screen. He was being wrenched from his foster family.

I lifted my hand off the divider and laid it gently in my own lap. I thought, maybe not. This isn't grade school. I don't need her to tell me who I am.

At the end of the movie I started clapping so hard my hands burned. I had been sobbing without realizing it. I could feel people looking over at us. I had gone past the point of stopping, like when you throw up so much that you get the dry heaves. I was sobbing so deeply that it sounded like a horse braying. A flash flood—everything that had happened with Asia in Tennessee, JT's story, Laura's story, and all of my yearning to be someone else, to be someone who Asia wanted, who other people respected, not just some kid, some stand-in, some puppet.

Laura got up, dragging me with her, and took me by the shoulders along the aisle. We went into a marble toilet stall. Uncontrollable sobs racked my body. She hugged me, and I held onto her torso like an inner tube.

"We've come so far! Shhh. Shhh," she whispered, holding the back of my head. I threw off my wig.

"It's so dark. It's like a punch in the stomach!" I wailed, trying to pin my tears on the movie.

"I know. I can't believe it came out of me." She was crying too. Her mascara ran down her face. Suddenly, she pushed me away so that she could look me in the eye, "I think you need to tell Asia how you felt about Tennessee."

"Why?"

I had no intention of doing that.

"I saw it. I saw you seal up. It's like when you have a sore, and it scabs over, but you still have all kinds of dirt underneath the scab. You still have shit under there. You need to go back in and take out that dirt."

My body tensed up.

"I can't do that. It's over between us. She's not going to change even if I talk to her." I wasn't into *processing*. And couldn't imagine Asia was either.

"But what about you?"

She pulled a towel off the counter, wet it, and leaned into the mirror rubbing the smears off her face.

A few minutes later, Laura and I emerged to find Asia waiting in the hallway, surrounded by a throng of moviegoers. I felt slightly embarrassed. People stared at me curiously, giving me that look: "Are you sure you're alright?" Somebody handed me a bar of chocolate. Everyone seemed like they needed a pick-me-up. A stiff drink. I didn't want all these people surrounding me, thinking, "Oh, the poor fucked-up little guy!" But they weren't going away. I kept at Laura's side, not making eye contact with anyone, just staring down at the floor. We left with the producers and had a bad dinner, then went to a crowded rooftop party, where the temptation of getting drunk floated by me in crystal goblets balanced high on silver trays. I resisted to keep my promise to Laura that I wouldn't drink. But I was hoping that I would see Asia and that we would hang out together. Instead, Laura and I ditched the party shortly after we got there.

The next day, I decided that I would talk to Asia after the press conferences were over. The first meeting was on a dock on a little stage, and a group of about fifty reporters sat down in front of us on fold-out chairs. Asia dangled one foot off the other and shook her hair into her eyes. She was less graceful in her movements than she had been last night. More twitchy, ready for battle. She wore jeans and a black short-sleeved sweatshirt with a leather cap on underneath the hood.

A reporter from *Variety* asked, "You delve into this poor child's life in such a way that it is almost exploitive, one horrific thing after another. Were you referencing Courtney Love?"

Asia cleared her throat, smiling a little and showing her teeth.

"You know, people keep saying this and it surprises me. I think it is the blond hair. And the punk-rock mother archetype. JT and I had been talking about this . . ." I guess we had. I couldn't remember the last time that I had talked to her about anything except telling her that she wasn't fat. She continued, "In the '50s we had the archetype of the stay-at-home mom. In the '60s it was the hippie mom. The '70s was the single, disco mom. And the '80s, well, we are just barely coming up on this archetype. And punk rock was one of the most profound subcultures. So people keep associating Courtney Love with the Sarah character because they don't know where to place her. The mother is not a black-and-white sort of character. I was interested in capturing that which was in JT's books," she points to me. "Those shades of grey. Sarah loves her son, but it is a complicated love. Ah," her voice collapses.

"She almost considers him a part of her, an extension, an appendage."

Spurred on by Laura's voice in my head, I chimed in. "Not everybody has the courage to make this story. It ain't like this hasn't happened to kids everywhere. You know, it's like . . . um . . . it's happened before. And it'll probably happen again. Like, in America, not just anybody can drive; they have to take a test. But anybody," this is how Laura had said it too, "anybody can have a child. They just pop 'em out, you know?"

The answer fell flat. They didn't believe me. I looked over at Asia. She didn't seem to be there with me either. That's it, I thought, I'm not saying anything else. Music echoed through the open door, then suddenly somebody addressed a question to me.

"JT, you claim that your fiction is based on true-life experience. And yet we have no idea who you are under your wig and sunglasses. Your voice, as well, sounds like a woman's . . ."

My stomach dropped. This, again.

A few months ago, I wasn't ready to answer this. Now I knew what to say with confidence.

"Yeah, I do. I mean, I could be. I could be anybody. I could be a two-hundred-pound black man in Idaho right now. It doesn't matter. My work is out there. Y'all know me through the work."

"JT, how did you and Asia discover one another?"

A safe enough question. Unfortunately, one I don't know the answer to. How had we met? I mean, I knew how *we* had met. But if I made something up she'd know it. How could I not know this? I could feel Asia staring at me.

"Um, uh . . . Well, uh."

Thankfully Asia jumped in: "A mutual, friend Billy Chainsaw, who lives in England, gave me JT's books to read. I was dumbfounded. I had never felt so akin to a book. I had never had that kind of reaction to a piece of literature. And then a funny thing happened: JT's Italian publishers contacted me to read his work at a literary festival."

"Then we spent weeks together in Italy. By the end, she asked me about making the books into a movie," I said.

"But he was very vague," she gave me a teasing look.

"Well, I wasn't sure, you know 'cause Gus had talked about taking some of the stories. I wanted to give it to her, though."

Another reporter addressed me, "JT, what do you think of the movie?"

"Well, I mean, I'm here, aren't I? I'm awestruck and totally flattered that she included me in so much of the process and paid such respect to the work. Went, like, above and beyond. Like getting this one particular fuzzy blanket with a lion on it that my mother had. And I think it's really a courageous movie, you know." Now say Laura's pipe thing, I thought. "Ever since I was a little kid, I wanted to attach a pipe from my head to someone else's so that I could share all those images with someone else, and I wouldn't be alone with them."

My voice faltered. Jesus, I thought, every time I speak I begin to cry, or I throw up.

"And so this has been a real blessed thing . . ." I trailed off.

The press went on all day. We had another round table, and then Asia's manager split us up, shuffling us from one reporter to another. The high afternoon sun reflected on the surface of the pool, a patchwork of reflection and refraction. I felt like I was in a board game. I worried that our answers weren't matching up. Laura, Geoff, and Thor hung out under the café awning adjacent to the pool. At one point, Laura had a plate of food sent over to me. I ate it in the sun without much revel, my fasting thwarted yet again.

At the end of the day, after the last interview, we all sat down in lawn chairs, slightly exhausted. I felt Laura asking me with her eyes, when was I going to talk to Asia? I looked over my shoulder and sighed. I reluctantly got up and went over and sat down next to Asia on her lounge chair.

"Um, can we talk in private?"

"Okay."

"Let's go over there," I said, pointing.

We walked to the opposite side of the pool. Everyone standing on the other side watched us. I could feel heads turning.

"Let's go to the bathroom," I said. It seemed that it had become the more appropriate setting lately. I felt JT's voice morphing into my own. I looked at her and took a breath.

"I just wanted to tell you that it really hurt me back in Tennessee when you and Mike were spending the night together—not that you guys shouldn't have been together. I mean, I just wish I hadn't been staying with you. It was just, like, awkward. And shitty. I don't know why you brought me out there in the first place."

She began to cry.

"And it's, like, I wouldn't have even mentioned it, but I guess it keeps coming up inside me, so I uh, I just wanted to tell you." I paused. "I'm trying to talk about my feelings more and not keep them bottled up."

She was still crying, then blubbering. I hugged her. It reminded me of the scene in *The Heart* when little JT takes his mother in his arms when they're dying their hair black in a public bathroom.

"And I really value you as a friend. As a friend most importantly. You're really amazing." There, I said it.

She caught her breath, swallowed, then growled, "I'm sorry I did that."

"I mean, it's okay. It's not a big deal. I wasn't looking for an apology. I just thought I should express it for *myself*. . . . For *me*."

TOKYO

WE SAT IN A RESTAURANT in a high-rise hotel with windows looking out onto the nightscape of Tokyo. The city stretched out flat before us, reminding me of a desert. The restaurant had Western style chairs and tables with screens partitioning each table. The night before we had been to a traditional Japanese restaurant, a honeycomb of blond wood rooms, where we each sat on a raised podium on indigo dyed pillows. As the waiters served three whole grilled and salted mackerels, an array of sashimi and sushi rolls, and blossoms of purple and dark green chopped seaweed, Asia entered the room.

She pivoted quickly around the corner of one of the screens. Behind her a boy followed with long brown hair and a healthy complexion. A musician type, wearing a pea coat and matching black low-top Converses and dark colored jeans. Asia's cheeks and nose were slightly flushed from the outside air. The film distributors of *The Heart* all stood up to welcome Asia and her friend to the table. Laura and I said our hellos less cordially.

Before going to Japan, Laura, Geoff, and I had been flown out to Italy again by JT's Italian publishers. Asia had agreed to attend the book events, then bailed on each one of them at the last minute. JT had always promoted her film work, and Laura was furious. I wanted to share in Laura's rage, but it was hard to muster. I felt, of course, it would have been nice for her to attend JT's events, since he had attended hers, but if she didn't want to she wouldn't. In fact, she hadn't. And as always, I was Switzerland, forever neutral.

As Asia came and sat in the chair next to me, I put out my hand amiably to her companion, Billy. Welcome to the club, friend.

"Hey, how's it going, man? Whad'ja do all day while we were in the tower?"

"Um, I actually got kind of lost on the subway. Felt like I was in a scene from *Lost in Translation*." I had to admit, he seemed like a sweetheart.

Asia and I had had interviews in the hotel back-to-back from nine to seven in the evening.

Our first interview had been on *Yo! MTV*. Laura had insisted that I wear a Thistle band T-shirt, even though I hated wearing T-shirts, especially ones with decals on them.

I hissed "I can't wear it! I won't feel comfortable. It's not my style!"

Why couldn't I wear something that made me feel good? Why couldn't I wear Costume National?

"Wear it for your brother!"

That shut me up.

Ukio* came over and handed us each Starbucks coffee cups. "Good morning," she said sweetly, digging out brown packets of Turbinado sugar from her pockets.

---

* I can't remember the names of the Japanese publishers and film distributors so these are made up.

I peeled off the plastic lid. A brown and white feather of foam graced the top.

A latte!

"I ordered that for you." Laura said, taking a sip from her cup, keeping her woolen Misfits gloves on.

"Thank you," I said tearing open the sugar. "Okay, I'll wear the fucking T-shirt."

Asia had passed by us without saying anything to either of us. She sat down on a couch where the next interview would take place. Two men came from across the room, conscientiously looking for the best place to mic her, as if tracing a map along her jacket.

"Here, wait. Let me take this off. I won't wear it during the interview."

As she took off her leather jacket, I saw that she wore a black Dominion* band T-shirt, with antiquated silvery white lettering.

Her T-shirt is so much better than ours, I thought.

Laura looked over at her, pointing a finger. "See, she knows the game."

Kiosuke signaled for me to come over, and I hurriedly pulled the T-shirt on over my collared shirt. I sat down next to Asia on the couch, wearily.

A video man with neat dreadlocks stationed himself in front of us, and the interviewee and translator stationed themselves next to him.

They started out with the usual set of questions about process, when the film would come out, and then advanced to more general topics.

---

* I can't remember the name of the band so I've made this one up.

"What kind of music do you like?"

"Well, y'all . . ." I pointed at my shirt like Vanna White.

"I've been writing music with my family, and I am so amazed by the power of it. The band is really good. Astor is like a musical God. And Speedie Two is the singer. It used to be Speedie One." I vaguely pointed in Laura's direction. She had given up singing and renamed her replacement.

"We just did a buncha shows in Italy, and it was awesome." I glanced over at Asia. "I just love that immediacy, man. It's like, here I am wasting away in this dark room, writing, and then I go into the kitchen and Astor's playing the guitar and Speedie's singing and the sun is shining through the window and the plants look happy. I don't get to see people's reactions for months, years, when I'm writing. But music! When I hear the band play live I feel so happy I want to cry."

Asia started, "I really love this band Dominion. They have a deep sound, very moody and rich. Their music is actually in the movie, one of the last songs. Beautiful."

"Do you both do yoga?" They just kept moving along. We answered in unison, "No."

Then Asia said, "I'm sorry, can we stop for a second?"

They stopped the camera. She motioned across the room.

"Can you get *her* out of my line of vision? I can't concentrate when she is . . . gloating over there at the wall."

Everyone was very quiet as Kiosuke ushered Laura out of the room. Laura could not say anything back, not in the middle of the interview. She just flashed a dangerous smile.

Later, as we settled into our seats at dinner, I felt queasy. Asia and Laura were both so strong-headed. Ukio, oblivious to the tension, explained to us what was in each dish as it was served. We all raised our chopsticks together and began to eat. Ukio pulled her long hair back to one shoulder, professionally poking at the mackerel, the skin as iridescent as mercury. She peeled off bits of brown flesh and placed it on our plates. The fish was oily and rich. The three film distributors spoke quietly, watching us eat with approval.

After we cleaned the plates of all the appetizers, Asia asked them, "Is it alright if I smoke?"

Kiosuke nodded, "Of course. You can smoke pretty much anywhere in Japan."

However, Laura said quickly, "No, oh no. Can you not? You know it makes me sick."

Laura's perennial battle when we travel abroad. It seemed that most of the world outside of the US smoked in their cars, at the table, really wherever they pleased. I knew it made her sick. Even so, I had trouble backing her up on this one. I loved being able to smoke everywhere.

Asia had already lit her cigarette as Laura exclaimed, "Please!"

Asia blew smoke in her face, growled, and tossed her napkin on the table. "Please, what?" She stared at Laura, the smoke curling in front of her face like an evil little question mark. Laura stared back, then said, "Why are you such a princess?"

"I don't need to sit with this shit." Asia said.

She stood up and in one flush movement was seated at another table. Billy loyally followed. We all finished our dinner, talking awkwardly as if trying to fill the empty chairs at the end of the table, pretending we couldn't hear their private conversation a few tables away. Everyone except for Kiosuke had no idea what the fuck was going on.

After dinner, I sidled over to Asia.

She sat with her shoulders squeezed together and blew some smoke at me. I looked over my dark glasses and said, "Please come back and sit with all of us. Please?"

Billy and I met eyes. He was sympathetic, yet powerless.

"No, I don't need to be bossed around by that woman. I don't need to have someone talk to me like that."

"Please, come."

"We could smoke outside after dinner," Billy said.

"Right. We can all smoke outside after dinner." I chimed in, gratefully. Billy was a keeper.

She got up and followed us. Her movements suggested she didn't trust her own judgment.

We all sat down, reunited again, as porcelain bowls of dessert arrived. Little powdered balls of mochi jiggled next to a scoop of green tea ice cream. They were topped with cubes of translucent jelly, red beans, and slices of Fuji apple cut into the shape of bunny rabbits.

I don't know who spoke first, and I can't remember what started their fight, but I do remember that it was within a few bites of the most perfect dessert I had ever tasted. And I remember thinking, can't you motherfuckers wait until after dessert? How am I supposed to enjoy this oasis of mochi with you people screaming at each other? I let the last of my ice cream melt on the back of my tongue, but felt no pleasure.

"Everyone is supposed to tip-toe around you? You blow

smoke in people's faces, and order people out of your sight, and we all should just stand by at attention? You run right over people! And you bailed on our book events because they didn't profit you in any way. You're a selfish little princess." Laura screamed.

Asia rolled her eyes and said with venom. "Fuck you. I couldn't go to the events in Italy last time. They were going to take my daughter out of my custody. Your events were fine without me. I'm promoting the movie—I made this movie for JT!"

I sighed and watched the agar jelly quiver. The fuji apples emitted a low moan.

Laura shouted, "But you made a commitment. And I think we know who you made the movie for, which is fine, but don't act like Mother fucking Theresa." Laura was pointing her finger at Asia now, and I could tell it bothered Asia. "You said you would be there. And you shamed us. And you shamed our publishing house. Everyone has washed their hands of you. You're always making yourself a victim. Poor Asia. But I know why you can't take care of your daughter."

"Don't you talk about my daughter. You don't know anything about me. How dare you bring my daughter into this!"

They had raised their voices another octave. Everyone around the table knitted their brows. Kiosuke tried to calm them down, "Now ladies, please!" but it was past calm. It was an avalanche of drama. Asia stood up and abruptly threw her chair over, screeching, "Fuck you!" in that scratchy pitch that only a heavy smoker can have, and stormed out of the restaurant.

Laura screamed after her, raising her head up to project

over the rice paper screen, "Because you're a fucking drug addict!"

Billy got up and mumbled, "Um, maybe we'll be back."

Suddenly I noticed Ukio's head drop down, and a tear fell into her bowl of ice cream. The salt left an indent in the melting green island. She lifted her head up, and said, "I don't understand why you all are fighting like this."

The restaurant had fallen silent.

Back in our hotel room, Laura and I changed and began flossing our teeth. She put one foot up on the stone bathtub.

"I feel this aggression towards her. But I know it all revolves around the dynamics I created myself. But I really could barely hold it in today. Like she really pushed me to my limits. I could have pulled the plug right then and there, I could have told her who I really am and had no qualms about it."

I could see how hard this was for her. "Well, and that she did it in front of everyone, that makes it so hard on you."

"And that's the thing, you know, she's making it so hard on all of us, and we have to keep face for the publishing company. That's the important thing."

We sat there cleaning our teeth. I was mulling over the day, aware of the impossible situation this was for each of us emotionally, and the tenuous situation we would have to face with tomorrow's day of press. But I also felt grateful for the connection I was feeling in the moment. "I love you. I really do. I feel like I'm learning so much about myself through this experience with you."

Beyond the window, snow swirled. Some flakes stuck to the pane while others melted on the glass. Laura went to the window. "I feel like I am with you, too."

I was surprised. What could she ever have learned from me? I was just a kid. "Really?"

She exclaimed, "Constantly. Constantly!"

Then Laura grew pensive. "You know, I don't feel like I belong here in Japan. I'm too tall, I speak too loudly. I feel like I am constantly freaking people out. And then with Asia pulling this shit on me on top of all that—it's just so hard because I feel like everyone is looking at me, thinking, 'What is her problem?' Like I shouldn't even be here."

As we lay down, turning out the lights in our room, Laura began to tell me stories about her childhood again. "I knew I had this talent. When the teachers weren't watching, I was always entertaining other kids. Occasionally this group of people came to scout talented children to film in our class, and the teachers were supposed to pick out the top kids to be featured. They never picked me. Sometimes I could feel this rage well up inside of me. I knew I was a leader; I knew I had something. Even the film crew witnessed me rallying the kids, making them all laugh. They recognized my potential, but I could hear my teachers dissuading them, picking out the cute little girl with the blond pigtails. It was then that I realized I would always have to work double time."

I leaned into the down pillows, my head sinking slowly into the crisp smell of clean cotton sheets. I could hear Laura plucking at her fuzzy blanket, kneading it and purring like a cat.

All of the sudden, I heard a tapping in the room, faintly, like someone clicking their knuckles on the wall. It playfully ricocheted over every wall, the ceiling, to the left and right. It picked up speed and then slowed down.

"There it goes," she said calmly.

"What is that?" I whispered.

"It won't hurt you. It just does that. When I was twelve I was having a really hard time. I was going to commit suicide. I was planning out the ways in my head, sitting in the room I shared with my sister. She had the television on. And all of the sudden I began to hear it. It would bounce around the room like this. I didn't believe in ghosts, though my aunt saw them all the time. I thought, maybe it's the sediment settling in the walls of the building. But do you hear the way it changes speed? I had my sister turn off the TV. And I said, 'Can you hear that?' But she couldn't hear it. So I brought my mother into the room. My mother listened, and she said she couldn't hear it either. But when she said, 'You can sleep with me tonight,' I knew she actually had heard it."

Laura sighed.

"After all these years I've come to know that it's my guardian. At times in my life when I really feel like giving up, it shows up. Other times it shows up when I am doing well, just to check in on me. JT is connected to it as well." She took my hand.

We lay side by side. The city lights pulsed through the window.

I heard it just that one time.

HOLLYWOOD

CARRIE FISHER MET US IN HER DRIVEWAY dressed in a navy cotton bathrobe and slippers. About a foot shorter than me, she wore her hair in a bob. She had a half-cocked grin, full of mischief. "I'm glad you're here," she said warmly, opening her arms out expansively. "How was your flight?" She motioned for us to follow, and led us down a path to a little bungalow nestled in some trees. Opening a creaking wood-framed screen door, she said, "This used to be Harper's room." She was referring to her stepson Harper, whose father is Paul Simon. She also has a daughter, Billie, from another marriage. "Make yourselves at home. I'll be right back down. I need to go speak with my assistant about a few things."

Laura as JT had been emailing with Carrie for months. They seemed to have an appreciation of one another's writing, and a similarly dark sense of humor. Carrie had offered to put JT up if he ever needed to come down to Los Angeles, and recently JT had received offers to write for a few projects in Hollywood.

We retreated into our room. The bed was covered with a patchwork quilt. A few framed drawings of pen-scratched cartoon birds were mounted on the walls. The iron-framed windows to the right of the bed overlooked a huge oak tree that was garlanded with Christmas lights. From its branches, someone had hung a sign that read: "It happened one night."

A cobbled path led up to Carrie's hundred-year-old whitewashed adobe villa. The house had once belonged to Bette Davis. Carrie showed us on a previous trip an old magazine with a picture of Bette Davis in the dining room being served bacon and eggs by a black butler.

Laura and I ceremonially exploded our suitcases. I combed through my clothes, thinking about whether I should change my outfit. Laura yanked out the gifts she had collected for Carrie: a solid dark chocolate turtle carved by Michael Recchiuti that he'd sent JT for writing a passionate review of his chocolates; a bathing basket, replete with a loofa and pungent soaps; an inflatable travel pillow; and a can of baked beans from Hogs Paw Arkansas.

Laura balanced the chocolate in her hand, weighing it thoughtfully, "Man, she better appreciate this turtle. It's hard giving this one up."

Suddenly, Carrie swung open the screen door. A tall Coca-Cola with lemon sweated in her hand. She exclaimed, "Jesus Christ, you guys have been in here ten minutes and it looks like a bomb went off!"

"That's our system," I said.

"What kind of a system is that?" Carrie looked at Laura accusingly. She held her Coca-Cola midair, shaking the glass in Laura's direction. "Aren't you supposed to be helping?"

Laura looked a little sheepish and said defensively, "I do help!" She waved her hands a little, like she was grasping for something but couldn't remember what. "JT, go on and give the lady her gifts. See, we busted open the bags so we could give you these things." Laura gestured at the pile of loot. "Notice, the chocolate turtle is heavy enough to leave an imprint on the mattress!"

Carrie softened her voice and said, "Aw, that's really sweet."

She sat down on the edge of the bed, going through the gifts. When she got to the travel pillow, she exclaimed, "Ooh, I needed one of these!" She began to blow it up animatedly. Then, in the middle of a big inhale, she squinted and paused. Her forehead pinched into a frown. "JT, you look like a scullery maid. Who's dressing you?"

I was wearing a renovated tablecloth.

Laura waved her hands again defensively and said, "I don't know anything about that. He wears what he wants to."

"She doesn't. I mean, I do." I said. I could feel Carrie trying to figure out what was going on here. Who was this Speedie, anyway? The Svengali of the family? The inept assistant? Or the exploitive social worker, dressing JT only in tablecloths? Was Speedie squandering all of JT's hard-earned money?

The pillow was blown up now, and Carrie tucked it behind her head, letting her neck loll back onto it. Pointing her finger at Laura, Carrie said in a clipped growl, "What's going on here? Where is the money going? JT, are you stuffing it under your mattress like we talked about?"

"No, he's not." Laura said.

"I'm not talking to you," Carrie said curtly. "JT, do you have a financial advisor? Are you a part of the Writers Guild?"

"No, he's not," Laura ejected.

"You're answering for him again! Why are *you* answering for him when *you* can't even help him with a simple thing like keeping the room in order?"

I started to cough. I had a hack for months. Laura had been nagging me to quit smoking, and every time I coughed she brought it up. Not this time.

"I mean, JT has an excuse! What's yours?" Carrie said accusingly. Laura opened her mouth in response, but then, uncharacteristically, she closed it.

Carrie said with exasperation, "You know what? Save it."

"Carrie, you're right. I completely agree. Everything you're hitting on is right. He needs help. Guidance. I can't be the one to do that for him. I am, in some ways, as broken as he is. That's how we found each other."

Carrie squinted her eyes and said to me, "Come upstairs, JT. I'm going to find something for you to put on."

She led me up the path to her house. It was dim and smelled of wood and leather. It was February, but a towering Christmas tree stood in the middle of the living room. We passed through the sitting room, where piles of manuscripts had been left on the coffee table. A half-eaten granola bar nestled on its wrapper. Carrie picked her way around the couch and showed me a secret doorway in the back of the room. She flipped a switch behind the door and showed me a tiny chamber full of psychedelic graffiti. She said, "I imagine that Billie, as she enters teen-hood, will soon hole herself up in here."

In her bedroom, Carrie led me into her closet and began to rifle through drawers. She threw a sweater at me. She rummaged around some more and pulled out a violet wool smoking jacket with red trim. "I had that made in Hong Kong; you can wear it while you're writing." She found some jeweled gold platform wedgies and said, "These could be very you."

I replied, "If I want to impersonate Bette Davis."

"Don't you want to get more feminine? I mean, isn't that what you are going for?"

"Not exactly." It was much more complicated than that, I thought sadly to myself.

Carrie was so warm and generous with me, which made me want to let my guard down, but of course that was impossible with the secrecy I needed to maintain. I tried to search for something that would let her know more of me than the others did, and in a moment of desperation, I blurted out, "Wanna see my new tits?" Then immediately feared this was a mistake. In the past I never would have dared, because I wanted to protect JT. And because I felt so ambivalent about my own body. But things were starting to change. I was starting to feel like I had nothing to lose.

She tilted her head a little to take a drag of her cigarette. Squinting, she asked, "When did you get them?"

"Recently."

I ushered her out of the closet and gently signaled for her to stay put. Then I sidled back into the closet and took off my tablecloth and binding. I picked up the sweater she had given me, planning to put it on immediately after my show. I trailed it behind me for a kind of burlesque effect. I came out and walked into her bathroom. She followed me. I thrust my chest out, walking around like a male peacock.

In her deadpan voice she said, "They're good."

I agreed. Maybe this was the beginning of something. Maybe Carrie cared enough to be JT's surrogate mother. Maybe JT and I could co-exist. JT had Savannah's body and personality—and I had his. We would meld together, maybe even grow old together.

Our first meeting in Hollywood was with a producer who wanted JT to write the script for a story about Joan Jett and the Runaways. Brian, JT and Asia's manager, had set up a few other meetings as well. It seemed that JT had been writing so many articles, and had gathered so much press, that he had become a part of the Hollywood vernacular. Producers had finally caught wind of who he was, what he stood for, and what his writing and reputation would bring to a project. Writing for Hollywood seemed to be the obvious trajectory for JT. Everything had been leading up to this. I understood the importance of these next few meetings for her. But I also wondered, how could this keep going once JT was offered work? Especially if he landed a contract for a serial TV show? That kind of work would require JT to be there in person. I suddenly felt very spooked: my life would vanish once and for all. I would be giving JT more than my tits. I would always have puppet strings attached to my arms, and Laura whispering what to say in my ear.

We met the first producer at a famous Jewish delicatessen. It was hot, and we spent twenty minutes looking for parking space. As we settled into a booth, the producer confessed, "I have to be honest, JT, I haven't read your books, just your articles. But I can tell you're a good match for this project." He was tan and bald, with bushy eyebrows and a casual business look. He wore a black sweater vest over a white button-down with rolled-up sleeves.

Laura took a sip of her ice water. "Well, the thing that you intuitively know from reading a little bit of his work is that JT always finds the emotional arc. He always digs in." She motioned to the creamy side of her under arm as if she were referring to her veins.

Brian added, "JT is on his way to becoming a household brand-name celebrity. When one reads his name, one knows that the project carries an edginess, a freshness, a hipness."

Laura nodded in agreement. "We knew JT had reached a new level when Coca-Cola offered to pay him to go to one of their parties. But, more than that, JT is interested in taking problems of spirit and soul and transforming them into craft. He is not interested in pop culture. He wants to write things that will withstand the test of time. Here's the question: Is there an emotional arc to the Runaways story?" Laura raised her hands, and fluttered them around like a pair of moths, letting them fall into the lap of her silk skirt. The producer raised his eyebrows, watching her hands plunge.

Laura went on, "You should read the books. You should start with *Sarah* and then graduate to *The Heart*. Actually, should you read *Harold's End* in between?" She looked at me as if for permission. From behind the glasses I agreed, yes, he should read *Harold's End* in between. I hadn't bothered to wear the wig today. I'd only bound my chest and thrown on Carrie's sweater.

He ruminated, "I think that there *is* an emotional arc between all the girls. I'm positive that there is. But JT, say six months from now you're writing it, and you fall flat— you say, 'I give up, there is no emotional arc'—you gave it your best shot, right? Then that's not a big deal. We believe in your work. I'm telling you, we're a good match." He motioned to all of us at the table. He repeated, "We *are* a good match."

Laura said, "Well, JT doesn't want to take on a project just because you think *maybe* it *might* work. I mean, why bother? Why expend all of that energy prying open a story only to find that there is no nut?"

"Fucking squirrels," I muttered, Laura and I giggled together.

The producer laughed along with us and said, "Right. Well, you got a point. But, my point is, JT, I'd like to work with you. And there are many nuts. And we can pry them open one at a time."

Brian drove us back to Carrie's around nightfall. All the way home, Laura and he plotted and planned excitedly. "JT's going big time."

"Before you know it, Hollywood will be rolling out the red carpet," Brian concurred.

"JT has been in touch with David Milch. I just fucking love *Deadwood*." Laura could switch from the third to the first person now without fear. Everything had become so casual. She continued, "*Deadwood* is like fucking Shakespeare. It's so good. I sent them an email yesterday."

"By the way, Brian, JT really wants to join the Writers

Guild," Laura said. "It was Carrie's suggestion. How do we go about it?"

"It's easy," Brian said, "You just . . ."

I sat in the back, letting my body shift and counterbalance as Brian raced up into the hills in his Audi. It all seemed so easy and seamless. Surreal even. Behind us the grid of Los Angeles began to ignite and glow red and orange.

In Carrie's driveway, we said goodbye to Brian, then trudged up to our little cabana. The screen door of the bungalow slammed behind us. We started to change, getting ready to head up to the main house to hang out with Carrie. Laura grabbed my arm and whispered, "Wait. How do you explain that sound?" She went over and swung the door open and shut a few more times with her eyes closed, leaning her body in, pulling the door open and closed in a slow rhythm. Outside, the crickets chirped loudly. In the oak tree, the signs dangled and the Christmas lights winked, their colorful light strangely reflecting on the dew-damp lawn.

By the time Laura and I made it up to the main house, several people were already relaxing in the living room. Carrie loved to have friends over. She had ordered a feast of Chinese food. Everyone who came over seemed at ease, without any of the awkward pleasantries or formalities of the parties I had come to know. It was like we were all staying with her; everyone was family.

We met Harper, who usually traveled around with his girlfriend Seven, a tiny girl with a hoarse voice; Charlie

Wessler, the producer of the Farrelly Brothers' movies; Al Pacino's ex, Beverly D'Angelo, who was dressed to the nines in a linen suit; and Sean, John Lennon's son. The doorbell rang and Sean Lennon introduced his date, a girl wearing a dress made out of handkerchiefs. He emptied Carrie's stereo and put on his new album, *Friendly Fire*, passing around the sleeve, which had a close-up of his face on it.

A tall man came in without knocking. He wiped his feet on the doormat. He had a bald head and dark features. He introduced himself as Bruce. He went over to Carrie and lifted her up from where she was standing. They began to sing a song about "Blowing me while I shit blood" in a cabaret style.

"I guess they're close," Laura said jokingly.

"Oh, they go way back," Harper said.

Harper said to Seven, "JT and I talked about making a song together."

I said, without even thinking about it, "I don't know if I can do that anymore. I know we had talked about that over the phone, Harper, but I don't think it's a good idea."

"We'll just sit down together, and it will all come out. It'll be fun."

"I don't know. We might have to do it over the phone," I said, feeling a little of the old nervousness flooding back. I couldn't write a song. That was Laura's arena.

"It'll be great." Laura exclaimed, slapping me on the shoulder. "You should do it by the pool tomorrow."

Okay, I thought to myself. Just go with it. "Alright, we'll give it a try by the pool."

Laura began talking to Bruce. They seemed to hit it off, talking and gesturing over their Chinese food.

Over his own soft voice playing on the loud speakers, I heard Sean say to the girl, "I wrote most of these really late at night. Come to think about it, it was morning in Japan."

Laura and Bruce emerged from the kitchen. Laura then went up to Carrie and whispered something to her.

"Really?" Carrie said with slight disdain.

I don't know what they talked about in the kitchen. It seemed that she wanted Carrie to know that her old friend had found something interesting and compelling in Speedie. I thought it socially awkward the way she went straight to Carrie to tell her. I also thought about Geoff, but I was in no position to judge. It seemed like Laura just wanted to redeem herself in Carrie's eyes, and enjoy herself. Laura and Bruce kept talking with grins on their faces. Laura kind of tittered and I saw Carrie roll her eyes tiredly.

As we watched an episode of *Deadwood*, Laura waxed on about the show and how brilliant David Milch, its creator, is. Switching the channel to *Lost*, Carrie began to tease her. She said, "You see that rock? That rock and I are very intimate over the phone. I was just out with that rock last Sunday!"

Laura's voice raised in pitch. "I didn't say that to name drop." Laura sounded frustrated.

Carrie said, "I don't mean to give you a hard time. It's just so easy to tease you."

Soon the group tired of watching television and moved into the living room to play games.

The television and Chinese food had put me in a torpid floating state. Before long I passed out in Carrie's bed, wrapped up in a long scarf. I woke up at five in the morning. A grey light glowed from the muted television set. A '60s globular love chair made out of see-through plastic swung quietly in the light of the Duraflame fire. I kicked off a throw that someone had laid over me. I tiptoed into the bathroom to wash my face, passing Carrie's sleeping body. Under her covers, she lay in deep sleep, breathing heavily, her eyes moving under her eyelids. I wet my face. The scarf left deep impressions around my neck. In the quiet I thought, cherish this moment. I am still me. I can still look out and see the world from my own lens. Soon I might forget how to do that. I contemplated whether I should head back to the bungalow. It seemed incredibly far away, so I climbed back into Carrie's bed and fell back asleep thinking about how I might wake up and feel ready to write a song with Paul Simon's son.

When I finally arose, the sun was streaming through the sliding door. It was eleven thirty in the morning. I wandered out to the living room, which was empty.

I heard music outside in the garden. Frank Sinatra. Opening the door, I caught sight of a brawny man in blue exercise shorts and a yellow polo shirt. His arms rested on his hips as he counted aloud, "twenty, twenty-one, twenty-two . . ."

On the floor, beneath the trainer, Sean was doing reps on his back. He moaned in his high voice. The trainer smiled and said, "Getting him ready for the *Friendly Fire* tour." Sean wore a sweatband, and his forehead was glistening with perspiration. He squirmed on the floor as the trainer nodded his head in time with another sit up, counting out, "Thirty-three . . ." Frank belted out, "That's why the lady is a tramp!"

Across the way, Carrie pedaled on a treadmill. She moved her head back and forth in synch with her legs, singing along, "Laaaady!" She had a Diet Coke and remote control next to her. The Olympics were on TV, muted. "There are chocolate chip silver dollar pancakes in the kitchen for you, Van Winkle," she said.

"Don't talk about those right now," Sean moaned.

Carrie lifted her hand off the treadmill and pointed at me emphatically. "And I'm taking you to the doctor for that nasty cough of yours."

I LICKED MY THREE-HUNDREDTH STAMP, my tongue heavy and thick from the glue. My friend Brenda and I were sending out announcements for our event in New York City. We had teamed up with several other independent designers and rented a lounge at the Sheraton, which was next to one of the big fashion trade shows. We were hoping to tempt buyers to look at our clothes.

My cell phone rang. The screen read, "private number."

"Hello?" I said, my tongue sticking to the roof of my mouth.

"Hello, Savannah." It was a man's low voice.

"Do you know who this is?" He had a heavy-handed manner, like a stalker from a B-movie.

I replied slowly, "No."

"It's Warren St. John." My stomach dropped. The *New York Times* reporter I'd met last year as JT was calling me by my real name.

"Okay?" I managed, after a second. I moved into the neighboring office. How had he gotten my cell phone number? Who would have given it to him?

"Is there anything you would like to tell me?"

My voice squeaked, "No."

"I have a picture of you, Savannah." His voice dropped an octave, "Without the wigs and sunglasses. I've been showing it to many of your intimates. They all agree that the person in the photo is JT." He paused, savoring what he had just said. He sounded threatening, so different from the first time when I had met him, when he had seemed sweet and open. He had dragged Geoff, Laura, Holli Pops, and me all over New York City for a late lunch. Everything was closed. Finally, he took us into a hole-in-the-wall sushi joint. The walls were painted mint green. He motioned apologetically for us to sit down.

Over rice bowls, I answered his questions in stilted shorthand. "Used to be Jeremiah. But then on the street my friends called me 'Terminator,' like in an ironic way. Then it morphed into JT." I picked up my limp hamachi and glanced at Laura.

She chewed and swallowed, then added, "JT told me that when he first started using his new initials, he sent a letter to Art Spiegelman, signed 'JT, a.k.a Terminator,' and Spiegelman sent a letter back to him signed 'The Ruminator.'"

Warren had written these details down avidly. Afterwards, we took him to watch Geoff's band, Thistle, rehearse in a room full of mirrors. He wrote a very positive two-page article for the *New York Times* style section.

On the phone, Warren continued, "Savannah, how old are you?" He seemed to enjoy saying my name.

"Turning twenty-five," I mumbled. JT and I were the same age, so this seemed safe to say.

"What?"

"Twenty-five," I said crossly.

"Well, I suggest you get a lawyer. People are angry. Many people are going to be angry." He enunciated, "The article comes out on Monday and people will demand an explanation. I suggest that you speak for yourself. Now, I'd like to ask you a few questions."

"I don't know what you're talking about," I said quickly. This was not the moment to begin speaking up as myself.

"I think you do," he replied. "You have until tonight." He began reciting his phone number.

I pretended to write down the number. I wondered about Laura. He must have called her first. Did she talk?

He repeated, "It would be in your best interest to answer for yourself. You are going to have a lot of angry people demanding an explanation, and you're probably going to face—"

"Look, I don't need this in my life right now," I interrupted.

Then I hung up on him. The phone rang again almost instantly, and I threw it on the couch as if it had bitten me. I fumbled to turn it off as it vibrated menacingly.

I called Laura from Brenda's phone.

". . . and then he told me to get a lawyer!" I squawked.

"Oh, don't listen to him. Did you admit to anything?"

"No, no. I don't think so," I said, sniffling. "Did he say that to you?"

"All the same kinds of threats, but catered to my life—what will happen to Thor, Geoff, my mother—basically the threats were tailored to be my worst nightmares. Listen, don't worry. You might not be JT anymore, but there is nothing that proves that you didn't write those books. Who says you couldn't have written them?" She said intensely. She still wanted me to say I had written the books? I was flattered that she thought I could have written them, but I was also confused. She thought we could still keep this thing going? "Can you come over in the morning?"

"Yeah," I replied, "I'll be there by ten."

I spent the night at Brenda's. As soon as I woke up, I rode over to Laura's apartment on my bicycle. It had rained the night before. I stopped to buy a cup of coffee and a copy of the *New York Times* along the way. At the deli I took a burning gulp of lousy coffee. I furtively glanced over my shoulder at the Pakistani guy behind the counter, who was watching an Indian musical and cracking pumpkin seeds between his two front teeth. JT had made the front page of the style section again. My fingers trembled slightly as I read Warren's article. Indignantly, I tucked the paper into my shoulder bag and continued on my way.

Ringing the bell, I waited for Laura to answer.

From the top of the stairs, she called, "Who is it? Hang on!"

"It's me!" I yelled, looking around.

She rustled the tie-dyed curtain at the base of the glass door, checking the tips of my shoes as always.

Obscuring her body with the door, she ushered me in quickly as if there were a strong wind blowing. Hugging me, she said, "Babyhead." Her hands slid down to my elbows and she sighed, "Maybe we should just pull the plug."

For lack of anything better to say, I whispered, "It's all part of the journey."

"At play in the fields of the Lord," she replied without missing a beat.

Then she changed tone. "Geoff's officially gone off the deep end. He's threatening to call Warren and to do a tell-all."

"No! That doesn't make any sense! Why?"

She looked up to the stairwell and said, "I don't know. He's really mad at me." Geoff had moved out a few months before. He had become fed up with the paradigm Laura had created in the house. He said he could no longer stomach living with JT. I could understand his feelings, but I couldn't believe he would really betray Laura, that he would call the *New York Times*. Eventually, he did, when it seemed like there was a possibility that Laura could keep JT alive after all.

"Is he here?" I asked.

"No, he came by yesterday and picked up his equipment. He was storming around the house, saying, 'The jig is up!' as if he were happy about it. He doesn't feel like the same person I once knew."

The teakettle droned. I followed her up the stairs into the kitchen. She swung open the fridge, one hand on her hip, and said, "The whole thing makes me revert into shame. I feel like I want to disappear." Then, with the old customary joy of offering, she said, "You want tea?"

"Sure, I'll have tea."

"You want food? We got apples. Or leftovers from the macrobiotic restaurant, some vegan chocolate pudding. I could make you eggs . . ."

I said quietly, "No, I can't eat right now. I'm okay."

"You're better than okay, Babyhead," she said, and smiled wistfully.

She pulled out the soymilk and placed it on the counter, bumping the door shut. "I got a lot of emails already. Some people are very clear about their intentions. It's going to be a witch hunt."

I watched her pour hot water into her stained Patriots mug. I wondered if everyone would really be as angry as Warren had suggested. The article had quoted a few people, and they certainly were angry. I thought about all the people we had met. And of course, I wondered about Asia. I suddenly remembered that the movie version of *The Heart* was going to be released in the US in just a few weeks. I thought with regret that I should have told her what we were up to that night at the Ritz, so that she wouldn't have to find out this way. Laura continued, "I feel like I saw this coming. Like it was all in *Sarah*. This is the hunt, the part at the end where the boy is naked in the woods."

I paused, trying to picture how the book ended, then laughed, "Couldn't JT have ended up lounging on a couch in a party dress, eating bonbons, and getting a foot rub instead?"

Laura snorted, then sighed deeply, tearing up a little.

"No, that would have been a dud ending."

I went over to the cupboard and pulled out the Cheat River mug, filling it with hot water, then followed her down the dark hallway to her office and settled myself into the torn cushions on the couch.

I pushed JT's stuff aside: a mess of loose paper, books and magazines, chocolate wrappers, and a trove of odd toys fresh in their boxes, which Laura always saved to give as gifts. In an attempt to organize the mire, Geoff had built a bookshelf, which stood loaded to the ceiling. He'd called Laura a packrat, saying that only someone who was mentally ill could live like this, and that he couldn't put up with it anymore. The maroon blinds were pulled shut, as always. The carpet was a landfill of receipts, coupons, and newspaper clippings. But I knew why she'd saved these little mementos; each was a fragment of JT's existence. Throwing out an article or a letter, for her, was like chopping off JT's hand or a piece of his heart and putting it in the trash.

Laura read aloud segments of the different emails she'd received since the *Times* article had come out that morning. Some friends had sent her notes of support, but most of the emails were accusing: "Laura, you exploited our sympathy to make yourself famous and to meet celebrities." CNN, BBC, the *Guardian*, and *Associated Press* had called. Steve Garbarino had offered to tell her story for *Vanity Fair*.

"Did you hear anything from Asia?" I asked.

She darted her eyes at me painfully and confessed, "She said . . . it's gonna be me and her walking the red carpet for *The Heart* premiere."

"Really?" I could hear my voice rising in pitch.

She quickly added, "I don't think we should go to that now, do you?"

"I guess not," I said, my throat burning with hurt. Now I knew how Laura had felt all those years when people had told JT to get rid of Speedie. This was what she had always tried to explain to me.

"Well, it's good she didn't care, right?" I asked in a tight voice.

"She was all business," Laura said, trying to be comforting.

"What do you think is going to happen?" I asked, hardly expecting an answer.

I wondered how Laura was going to emerge in the world without JT shielding her. The glow of the screen reflected on her pale complexion.

"I think we can keep it going," she said reassuringly. She seemed to be talking more to herself than to me. "Like I said, nobody can prove that you didn't write those books. You would tell them you wrote them, right?"

"Um, yeah, I guess so," I said. Though it seemed crazy to me. Her willfulness amazed me. What I saw as a sinking ship, she saw as a small leak that she could patch up.

We should have known the end was near when, a few months before, *New York Magazine* published an article titled, "Who is the Real JT LeRoy?" Stephen Beachy, the writer, was convinced that Laura had created JT. He wrote that the one missing bit of information was the identity of the person who played JT. I was coined as "Wigs and Sunglasses." When the article came out, I had wondered if JT could go on with his life as if nothing had happened. Oddly enough, he could. He continued to write his restaurant reviews and monthly columns. Laura didn't let JT go down to Los Angeles as often, but in many ways she seemed emboldened by the truth. Again, her "Chinese Finger Puzzle": always go in further to get out.

When the *New York Magazine* article came out, dozens of JT's friends spoke up on his behalf. I groaned when I read the blogs of support, thinking to myself, it's going to be messy when the truth comes out. The last thing Laura and I did while I was JT was meet Robert Wilson, the avant-garde playwright and stage director. He invited JT to sit for a video portrait. Laura walked in with a curtsy and introduced herself to everyone as JT, and we all laughed, seemingly shocked and amused.

We didn't prepare for JT's unveiling. We didn't want to.

The doorbell rang. I sat on the couch, still focused on the paper piles littering the floor. Laura glanced from her computer to me. She stood up slowly, then moved cautiously toward the stairs. She was wearing oversized blue-plaid pajamas and a crew neck sweatshirt. Her shoulders were hunched protectively. I could see the back of her neck protruding from her collar as she sang out, "Who is it?"

A strong, confident voice called out, "I'm a reporter from the *San Francisco Chronicle*. I'm looking for Laura and Geoff."

Laura turned and whispered to me, "I used to work out with her at the gym." I imagined a woman wearing an exercise suit, waiting downstairs at the gate. Laura adjusted the woolen nightcap that she always wore in the house, pulling it lower on her forehead as if she were a soldier preparing for battle. She replied loudly, "They're not here. They moved to Mendocino."

"Do you know a number I could reach them at?"

Laura issued her fax number.

She yelled, "I'm sorry there was a car passing by, will you say it . . ."

Laura hollered out the numbers, this time adding, "Get them! They should be brought down!" Her eyes shined.

I shuffled on the landing. "I don't think that's a good idea," I said anxiously. But Laura couldn't pass up these kinds of opportunities. Punk was punk.

The reporter said, not yelling this time, "Could we have a chat? I have some wonderful pastries with me."

Laura countered quickly, "No, I'm very busy right now." We both looked at each other, mouthing, "Pastries?" The woman had not done her research.

"Well, if you change your mind, here's my number. I'm slipping it under your gate." We listened as a few cars passed by.

Laura drawled, shucking her arm animatedly, "I'd give up mah whole life story for a pastry!"

As I was saying goodbye to Laura, I reassured her that I'd call if I noticed anyone staked out in someone else's drive-way. I pulled out my bike, seeing no signs of reporters. But as I rode downtown, I noticed a helicopter suspended in the air a couple of blocks away. As I turned, it veered in the same direction as I was going. I rode down a one-way street, straying from my usual path. The helicopter was like a hunting dog changing direction with its nose. I made a U-turn, cautiously crossing the trolley tracks, and ducked into a little knick-knack shop called The China Bazaar. Inside, I could hear the chopper's drone over the chirping of the auto crickets. A row of Disco Jesuses shimmered like a mirage. I dialed Laura on my cell phone. "Hey, it's me. I feel like there's a helicopter following me."

"What do you mean? When did it start following you?" she asked.

"I think it had been staked out at your apartment."

"Shit! I knew it! Listen to your instincts."

I snapped my phone closed and turned, startled by a slight man in slippers behind a counter. I pretended to consider green plastic strainers. I smiled at him, and he returned a nod. I retrieved a stick of bamboo from a bin. The bamboo was wrapped in a plastic pouch filled with what looked like baby jellyfish. I tilted it up for a closer look, and the man said, "For good luck." As the helicopter noise seemed to dissipate, I put it down and slipped out of the store.

As I arrived at my building, I passed a couple of guys mending the ornate brass grillwork in the foyer. I asked Will, the doorman, "What's that helicopter about?"

One of the repairmen, balanced on a ladder, answered before Will had even looked up from his paper. "Bomb scare down at the Civic Center."

"Oh," I said, feeling slightly disappointed and alarmed by my own paranoia. "Has anyone come by for me?"

Will picked a greasy chicken wing out of a shallow ging-ham-checked pail and started to chew on it. "Nope. Not a soul."

"If a woman comes by asking for me, will you tell her that I'm not here?"

Will licked his thumb and index fingers and smudged them on the sports page. He looked at me, and said casually, "Sure. I can do that." I kind of hoped that he would ask me why, but obviously he didn't care. I guess he wasn't reading the *New York Times*.

I walked slowly up the stairs and into my office, relocking the office door behind me. I lay down next to an iron burn on the polyester carpet and stared up at the ceiling. If somebody, another reporter or an angry fan, came by and knocked on the door, I would lie still and wait for them to leave. I had no idea what to say.

I wanted to simplify my feelings by telling myself neatly and without regret that I was glad it was over. The whole experience had been a contagious lie, one that spread and complicated and obstructed what I wanted my life to be. I shook my head and thought, "What a relief to be done with it!" No more excuses about why I couldn't make it to work. I would no longer have to tell the Capoeira group that I couldn't show up for the performance, again, because of a root canal, or a doctor's appointment. After all the lies, I knew nobody really believed my excuses. They just knew that I was unreliable. Living a double life had spread me thin. I had put being JT—which I had cautiously agreed to in the beginning, and which I thought would only be a one-time experiment, or an occasional outing—at the top of my list. Why had I done that? Being JT meant living in the moment. It was an exciting reprieve from real life. He had access to a world so beyond what I thought could be my own. And his pain was fully acknowledged, and embraced, by everyone who crossed his path. I sighed deeply as I admitted a deeper truth to myself: JT's contradictions were now my own. I had come to rely on him to push the limits of who I was. And I had become so addicted to it that I didn't know how to live without him.

It's strange to think of how much energy people poured into JT's existence. And through their collective energy, it was as though JT had come into being, separate from Laura or me. No wonder people felt betrayed.

JT had funneled emotions and thoughts between Laura and me as if through an invisible pipeline. It had become much more satisfying to triangulate our lives. In a sense, Laura, JT, and I had found a whole new way of communicating. Now our trinity was severed. Really, I was preparing to mourn the loss of two people. I worried that since JT was gone, Laura was soon to follow. I had worried when she said she wanted to disappear. I wanted her to find a way to live as herself and be acknowledged as a writer. I also worried that our friendship was over. Now that we weren't connected through JT, she wouldn't want me anymore. She would leave me behind. A part of me wished that I had walked away first. But I would never have been ready to say goodbye to him; it would never have been the right time. In truth, I had no idea what my life would be about without JT.

On the floor in my office, I felt a warmth in my crotch, and I realized, stunned, that I had started my period, which I wasn't expecting. I lay there feeling paralyzed. After years of complaining about how JT had distracted me from my life, I now had to face myself and my fears of failure, and create something on my own. I looked gratefully at the pins stuck in the carpet, the knots of thread and scraps of fabric littering the floor. Tomorrow morning, I thought, I will copy out the sizes for a pair of pants and a shirt pattern. I will source the fabric and buttons. I will miss JT. And I will hold him dear as I learn to live as myself.

ACKNOWLEDGMENTS

I would like to thank the people in my life who made this book possible: Hennessey, Sharon, Laura, Geoff, John, and all of the family and friends who supported me through this time. A special thanks to Mary Ellen Mark.

Thank you to Mick Rock, Juergen Teller, and Angela Scrivani.

And to those who helped in the process of creating *Girl Boy Girl*—Martha Kaplan, Amy Scholder, and everyone at Seven Stories Press—thank you for believing in me.

Savannah Knoop is a New York–based artist, writer, and filmmaker who has performed and exhibited at venues such as the Museum of Modern Art, the Whitney Museum, and the Institute of Contemporary Art in Philadelphia. They adapted their memoir *Girl Boy Girl: How I Became JT LeRoy* into a feature-length film, co-written and directed by Justin Kelly, and starring Kristen Stewart, Laura Dern, Kelvin Harrison Jr., Jim Sturgess, and Diane Kruger. *Girl Boy Girl* is their first book.